PROFIT
STRATEGIES
FOR
BUSINESS

ROBERT RACHLIN

A SPECTRUM BOOK

PRENTICE-HALL, INC., Englewood Cliffs, New Jersey 07632

Library of Congress Cataloging in Publication Data

Rachlin, Robert, 1937-
    Profit strategies for business.

    (A Spectrum Book)
    Includes bibliographical references and index.
    1. Business enterprises—Finance.   2. Capital
investments—Evaluation.   I. Title.
HG4026.R33 1981   658.1'55   80-27743
ISBN   0-13-726216-7
ISBN   0-13-726208-6 (pbk.)

©1981 by Prentice-Hall, Inc., Englewood Cliffs, New Jersey 07632

A SPECTRUM BOOK

10   9   8   7   6   5   4   3   2   1

Printed in the United States of America
Editorial/production supervision and interior design by Cyndy Lyle
Manufacturing buyer Cathie Lenard

Prentice-Hall International, Inc., *London*
Prentice-Hall of Australia Pty. Limited, *Sydney*
Prentice-Hall of Canada, Ltd., *Toronto*
Prentice-Hall of India Private Limited, *New Delhi*
Prentice-Hall of Japan, Inc., *Tokyo*
Prentice-Hall of Southeast Asia Pte. Ltd., *Singapore*
Whitehall Books Limited, *Wellington, New Zealand*

CONTENTS

iii

INTRODUCTION

The process of managing a business provides the opportunity to develop strategies necessary for the improvement of operations. These strategies take many different forms, since businesses operate differently due to philosophy, economic conditions, organizational chemistry, and business environment. However, whatever the influencing factor(s), it is apparent that certain basic strategies are needed to assure that a business will be profitable, and be able to meet its stated objectives. To this aim, this book will review some of those strategies.

This book will provide the business executive with tools for reviewing the business from different vantage points. There is no one simple way of reviewing performance and establishing objectives, but rather a series of reviews capable of guiding the executive through the many facets of an ever-changing business. These exercises are designed to bring into focus the many areas that require business decisions. Different segments of an organization require different types of business decisions. However, each of these business decisions relates to the overall company objectives, and must provide favorable action to link together total objectives. If one link fails, pressures are exerted on other parts of the organization to absorb those weaknesses. In some companies, the failures can be absorbed easily, while in others, severe consequences result.

To understand the total business concept, it is necessary to review what I call business strategies. The first chapter reviews the type of organization structure, i.e., investment vs. profit centers, used as a basis for evaluation. As part of that process, establishing target rate criteria is explored. Such evaluation techniques as the weighted cost of capital and its utilization, and the concept of return-on-investment highlight the evaluation processes needed when establishing business strategies.

The organization is looked at in detail by reviewing the consolidated balance sheet and the consolidated statement of earnings. This will provide the basis for reviewing the components of return-on-investment, namely, the turnover rate and the profitability rate. Within each component, decisions can be made to increase the factors, and ultimately, increase return-on-investment. A detailed analysis is presented showing the impact of various decisions and ways of improving profit performance.

Strategies Through Analysis attempts to analyze both financial statements through performance barometers called ratios. A segmentation of ratios is developed, aligning ratios with those functions needed to manage the total business, and reflected in the consolidated balance sheet and the consolidated statement of earnings. They are referred to as performance ratios, managing ratios, and profitability ratios. Each group measures different areas, and is summarized into a financial ratio matrix.

Strategies for controlling cash form an important role in business decisions. The source and application of funds highlights strategies that increase cash, or decisions that decrease cash. This is accomplished through the source and application of funds statement, and reflects changes in working capital. Through this process, earnings are also impacted in many ways.

Understanding how costs occur is paramount to understanding the business. Cost behavior will reflect how earnings are effected, and why. Types of costing methods are explored, such as absorption vs. direct costing, in which decisions change depending upon the method used. Understanding and analyzing the items that make up gross margin provides business managers with one of the main ingredients in generating earnings, namely, revenues and cost of sales.

Product line strategies are measured in terms of how many units are necessary to cover fixed costs, or breakeven, and how much is contributed by each product, i.e. product contribution. The need to maximize product mix to obtain higher earnings is fully explained. This approach provides the basis for decision-making by product, and will assist in establishing pricing, and should be used heavily in budgeting, planning, and controlling the business.

Capital spending strategies influence or impact the future earnings of the business. It is through this process that long-range plans are estabished, and strategies developed for operating the business. The process, objectives, variables, cash flow concepts, and methods of evaluation are fully explained. Without a sound capital program, progress and financial stability may be severely impaired.

As a final chapter, the area of reporting is explored. Reporting methods, types of reports, basics of reporting, and the need for accurate and current workable information will be expounded.

This book will highlight various review and control mechanisms for establishing strategies to control and improve the profitability of a business. It will not provide all the answers, but will develop enough understanding and knowledge, so that pertinent strategies can be applied to most businesses. However, it must be recognized that refinements may need to take place to meet certain types of businesses, as well as organizational philosophies. With this understanding, it is now possible to establish the necessary criteria for profitability strategies.

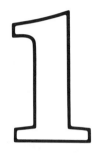

BUSINESS STRATEGIES

In a profit making organization the primary objective is to provide an adequate return to the investors by maximizing the funds entrusted to the company by the owners. The management must allocate those resources to maximize profits in both the short-term as well as the long-term, without assuming any unnecessary risks.

Maximizing investors' return can be accomplished through a combination of profit maximization and effective utilization of investment. Profit maximization is reflected by improving margins through increased revenues and better control of cost of production. In addition, decreasing operational costs will also result in higher profits. The effective utilization of capital can be reflected by using all assets to generate higher profits. For example, reducing excessive inventories by eliminating obsolete goods and increasing turnover; keep receivables down to an acceptable level; and reversing unproductive investments in plant and equipment. These actions will result in higher earnings, higher return-on-investment, and a business better able to withstand troubled times. This will be explored in later chapters.

4

INVESTMENT CENTERS VS. PROFIT CENTERS

In evaluating segments of a business it is important to distinguish between an investment center and a profit center. While both concepts deal with earnings generation, the investment center concept deals with the necessary expenditures to produce earnings. Both earnings and investments can be evaluated either in total, or as incremental additions or deletions to investment and/or earnings. In both cases, it is important to focus and evaluate the impact that earnings and investment have on each other. To state it another way, how much investment is needed to generate anticipated earnings, or what anticipated earnings can be expected from a given amount of investment?

Investment Center Concept

Favorable earnings alone do not always measure favorable peformance. In some cases, earnings may require a disproportionate amount of investment to generate those earnings. When measured by investment, a lower return-on-investment may in fact be produced, thus indicating an unfavorable relationship between earnings and investment. The key to successful management is to use investments productively to generate the highest possible earnings. This offers a more realistic approach to performance measurement.

If we look at hypothetical financial data for two periods, you can see how earnings and investment relate to each other, and the impact on return-on-investment. In this illustration, total assets will be used as the investment base.

Earnings Statement

	19X1	19X2
Net sales	$140,000	$168,000
Operating expenses	119,000	139,440
Operating profit	21,000	28,560
Other expense	700	—
Taxes	9,700	13,760
Net earnings	$ 10,600	$ 14,800

Balance Sheet

	19X1	19X2
Current assets	$ 62,000	$ 68,000
Net fixed assets	38,000	39,500
Other assets	5,000	5,500
Total assets	$105,000	$113,000
Return on assets	10.1%	13.1%

5

Note how more effective year 19X2 was over 19X1. Earnings increased 39.6%, while total assets only increased 7.6%. The results were three percentage points higher return-on-investment. You can see what impact a 7.6% increase in total assets had on earnings, and the relationship both earnings and investment had to each other. The results are shown as higher return-on-investment.

The investment center concept takes into consideration both elements of earnings and investment in an effort to reflect the necessary support to produce earnings on that business segment. The profit center concept will not include investment.

Profit Center Concept

This concept measures only the earnings of the business by evaluating segments that have both revenue and expense responsibility without the impact of investment. The profit center is sometimes referred to as the accountability or responsibility center. However, when any of these terms are used, it is advisable to internally define what is meant by accountability and responsibility, and to what extent managers are given the responsibility and authority to carry out accountability management.

Referring to the previous example, the profit center concept would be measured on net earnings. One measurement criteria would be net earnings as a percent of net sales. This would reflect the earnings generated by each dollar of sales. The following calculation results:

	19X1	19X2
Net sales	$140,000	$168,000
Net earnings	10,600	14,800
% of net sales	7.6%	8.8%

This calculation can also be computed on a before tax basis, such as operating profit on both a total operation, product line, location, or any other determinable way to measure performance. Keep in mind that, whatever method is used, the same measurement concept must be consistently used to arrive at a comparable evaluation.

SUMMARY

To properly measure performance along organizational structures, heads of reportable segments must have the authority and maintain significant influence on the segments used in the measurement, namely, net sales, earnings, and investment. This also means that control over expenses is possible and reflected in the end result which is earnings.

However, it is possible to measure an organizational unit as an entity, even though total control and influence are not directly present. This concept can be acceptable, but consideration must be given to measuring performance dependent upon the agreed level of accountability and the responsibility that is established. This criteria must be estabished and agreed upon in advance, and caution exercised to measure performance based on those responsibilities charged to the individual and/or unit. Measuring total performance without total responsibility can lead to improper evaluation and incorrect decisions.

ESTABLISHING TARGET RATES

The establishment of target rates that are workable, attainable by internal management, and measureable against similar outside businesses, presents a very real problem to management. While many companies have been evaluating operations for many years, the ability to establish acceptable target rates as a major decision-making tool remains a problem requiring much review. There are many criteria for establishing target rates. Some of them present the base from which overall target ratios are established. Some present the opportunity to establish target rates for segments of the business, while others establish insight as to where improvement opportunities exist, and where operations do not meet the operating objectives of the company. Whatever the outcome, or whatever the method used, it is important that strategies be developed for establishing target rates.

Target Rate Criteria

The following target rate criteria are by no means the only methods used, but will provide some understanding as to how target rates may be established.

☐ *Business, industry, or competitive conditions*—reviewing the environment in which you operate will provide a basis for establishing a recognized target rate. Most comparisons are made between like industries and help the community (stockholders, competitors, and financial institutions) to evaluate how well your company compares to the industry, individually or collectively. To maintain leadership, both in product and financial position, a company must be able to compete with others in the industry, thus providing the marketplace the incentive to invest in a company, and provide the needed funds to sustain and/or expand as needed.

☐ *Rate of return*—providing a rate in keeping with overall objectives such as potential, past performance, industry performance, etc.

☐ *Rate of return plus an additional percentage*—same as above, with an additional percentage added for growth.

□ *Past performance*—rate based on past performance of overall company or of accountability center.

□ *Cost of capital*—used as a cut-off, or target rate for overall performance and/or capital investment rate criteria.

□ *Future potential*—rate established based on future potential of the operation. Not necessarily representing an attainable rate.

□ *Risk*—higher risk operations generally establish higher target rates for both overall company and accountability centers.

□ *Other*—other criteria may be identified such as government regulations, environmental limitations, etc. Some of the above may be combined or variations established.

As you can see, various ways exist to establish target rates. These rates can be applied to profit centers as well as investment centers, although the investment center concept is preferred. Target rates can be applied in many different ways:

All investment centers and/or profit centers may be expected to earn the same rate. This is preferable only where operations are similar in nature, such as products, markets, distribution, etc.

Investment centers and/or profit centers are assigned different target rates based on the potential and experience of the center. This method is preferred since in many companies, most operations have differing profit potential. The ability to assign differing rates resulting in overall objectives will depend upon management style, and the ability of the management to maximize earnings. Further chapters will deal with this issue.

Some companies prefer not to use either the profit center or the investment center concept, and therefore will establish target rates only on the total operation. Caution is needed with this method, since overall evaluation may not highlight areas of least profit and areas of greater profit. Using this method objectives may be difficult to establish, since areas in which resources are needed may be difficult to identify.

WEIGHTED COST OF CAPITAL

Cost of capital represents an average rate of earnings which investors require to induce them to invest in a company and provide the needed capital for investment purposes. This cost can be measured many ways, i.e., as an opportunity cost, incremental cost, or as a weighted average cost. This discussion will deal with the weighted average cost since it is more difficult to compute, and is most commonly recognized as a tool for setting objectives.

When discussing cost, the question arises as to whose cost are we measuring. Is it managements' or is it the stockholders'? It is generally concluded that it is the stockholders', since they are investing because they expect to receive some benefits in the future. These benefits can be considered equivalent to what they would receive had they invested in some other investment alternative. The benefits they seek and which induce them to pay a price for the stock are future dividends and/or capital appreciation. Both of these benefits are derived from future earnings per share, and can be considered the principal factor affecting the price of a stock in the long-run. Therefore, part of this cost can be measured by the inverse of the price-earnings ratio, or the earnings-price ratio.

The price-earnings ratio can be considered a reflection of investor confidence. For example, when people are optimistic about the future and anticipate corporate profits to increase, they bid the price of the stock higher, thus raising the P/E multiple. When they have doubts about the future, or find more attractive investment opportunities, the investor will stay out of the equity market, and declining prices will result reducing the price-earnings ratio. It is this investor feeling that can impact the availability of capital needed to maintain the necessary growth and keep the company adequately financed.

Calculation

The stockholders view earnings retained in the business, or retained earnings, as an opportunity cost. When these monies are retained in the business, they cannot be used elsewhere to earn money. In theory, the retention of earnings is the same as if the dollars had been paid in dividends and were then used to buy more of the company's stock. Therefore, it reflects money which the stockholder has involuntarily invested in additional ownership of the company. It can be assumed that retained earnings has a cost and can be measured along with other equity amounts as follows:

$$\frac{\text{Anticipated earnings}}{\text{Net price per share}}$$

or

$$\frac{\text{Dividends per share}}{\text{Net price per share}} + \begin{array}{c}\text{expected annual rate of} \\ \text{growth of dividends}\end{array}$$

Using the following assumptions, the cost of equity is as follows:

Projected earnings per share	$3.00
Current net price per share	$30.00
Dividends per share	$1.50
Annual growth rate of dividends	5%

or

$$\frac{\$3.00}{\$30.00} = 10\% \quad \text{or} \quad \frac{\$1.50}{\$30.00} + 5\% = 10\%$$

The 10% cost of equity means that management must invest its earnings retained in the business, such as for capital investments, at a rate that will earn at least 10%. This rate will be part of the cost of capital calcualtion as follows:

Capital Structure	Total	After-Tax Cost	Weight	Weighted Cost
Long-term debt	$24,000	4%	30.4%	.01216
Preferred stock	1,000	5%	1.3	.00065
Common stock	19,800			
Capital surplus	6,000			
Retained earnings	28,200			
Common Equity	54,000	10%	68.3	.06830
Total Capital	$79,000		100.0%	.08111

Use of Weighted Cost of Capital

The weighted cost of capital rate of 8.1% reflects the weighted cost of all components of capital. Its primary use is to establish the minimum cut-off rate for new investments. Different rates can be established for varying risk elements, such as low cut-off rates for low risk projects, and high rates for high risk projects. In addition, these cut-off rates can also be applied for establishing investment/profit center objectives. It is suggested that while the weighted cost of capital serves as a minimum cut-off rate, additional percentage points should be added to reflect any contingency that may occur. For example, not all capital projects are cost saving or profit producing. Therefore, the realistic rate of capital investments must be established at a much higher rate to make up the difference of other capital investments not generating an acceptable rate of return. In addition, this rate also provides sufficient returns to offset poor performance years. Therefore, the cut-off rate of 8.1% may be in fact 10.1%, or an additional two percentage points built-in for contingencies. Caution should be given not to raise the contingency too high, so as to put the company in a position where profitable opportunities are rejected due to excessive contingencies. A reasonable percentage is suggested based on historical data.

Consequences of Not Meeting Cost of Capital

When a company consistently earns less than its cost of capital, several consequences occur. Different companies will react differently and with different time spans. However, it can be generally accepted that the following events will occur.

As companies earn less than their cost of capital, earnings will begin to decrease. When this occurs, dividends are reduced, and the company's growth is slowed down. This forces the company to provide a larger proportion of its capital needs by external financing. With higher external financing, earnings may continue to decrease, since external financing generally is more costly.

With earnings declining, both the stockholders' returns and expectations are reduced, which reflects in a lower market value of the stock. Capital costs continue to increase. The company continues to assume more risk, and the stock becomes less competitive. Financing costs continue to increase as well as capital costs.

While this situation may seem dramatic, it nevertheless emphasizes the importance of meeting the cost of capital rate. Over an identified period of time, the consequences as outlined will occur, but this will vary by company.

DECISION STRATEGIES

As previously discussed, the primary objective of a profit making organization is to provide an adequate return to the owners of the business while building or maintaining a firm foundation. The owners may represent stockholders, partners, or sole proprietors, or any other business arrangement. Through this process of providing an adequate return, management is constantly faced with a wide selection of possible investment alternatives. Therefore, it is safe to make the assumption that one of management's most important functions is the selection of investment opportunities to provide the most profitable alternative by investing those resources to which they are entrusted.

This process of increasing owner's investment can be accomplished by:

Utilizing those resources to maximize both short and long-term profits.

Obtaining the highest possible return on resources, without assuming any undue risks.

Producing the highest possible return through the process of effectively allocating resources.

While these are general goals most companies strive for, it is nevertheless important to establish them as they influence decisions. By establishing these general goals, it is possible to further identify how owner's return can be increased through some very basic operating actions. These operating actions will result in goals that profit-making organizations will establish resulting in increased owner's investment. The goals are to maximize profits through higher sales, increased margins, and controlled operational expenses. The other operating goals would be to effectively and productively use the investment of the company by such actions as deleting obsolete and stagnant inventories, but maintaining the proper balance to service customers; improve credit and collections policies to decrease receivables; and invest in fixed assets where adequate justification and/or return is obtainable. Further discussions will be made in later chapters.

In reviewing the above operating actions, it is apparent that this strategy provides the base for establishing measurement tools using return-on-investment.

Most operating actions in the organization will have some impact on return-on-investment, in that both profits and investments are reflected in the two financial statements, the balance sheet and earnings statement. Most decisions which can be measured on a numerical basis will find their way into the two mentioned financial statements. It is therefore important to highlight return-on-investment, and show its relative importance in the decision-making process, while keeping in mind that it is one of many measurement tools for evaluating performance.

ROI—A STRATEGY TOOL

Return-on-investment is one concept that embraces all parts of management at all levels. In order for the concept to be effective, management must be completely involved, since return-on-investment performance results from participation from all disciplines, at all levels, and is considered everyone's concern. The concept assists in maintaining growth by using historical performance to anticipate future performance. Its acceptance as a measurement tool has been and continues to be recognized by investors, the business community, the financial community, and most students of business concepts.

Why Use Return-on-Investment?

Management must have an easy method of reviewing past and future performance which results in a simple and understandable mathematical calculation. The return-on-investment concept offers this by measuring past performance and future investment decisions in a reasonably systematic manner. But, keep in mind that the basic assumption is that the best investment is one that maximizes profit. Its value lies in the fact that it enhances decision-making by providing the framework to do the following:

Forces more detailed planning.

Assists in eliminating decisions based on intuition, and presenting them in more realistic terms.

Aids in providing the structure to evaluate investment opportunities by establishing the necessary policies and procedures.

Measures management performance.

Creates an environment in which to respond to the marketplace.

As you can see, the vitality and direction of a company can vary very much depending on how return-on-investment is used, and the degree to which it is integrated within the organization. Full integration is established by coordinating all the uses and applications within the organization, so that whatever the use or application, the same return objective is constantly strived for. These major uses and applications are as follows:

External measurement—used as a basis for measuring external performance as compared to the internal organization. For example, comparisons between competitors and industries provide the basis for measuring how a company competes within its environment, and also in establishing long-range objectives.

Internal measurement—how internal segments perform and ways to improve performance. This includes divisions, investment centers, profit centers, product lines, etc.

Improve asset utilization—ways of maximizing profit through greater efficiency of use of assets such as cash, inventories, receivables, and fixed assets.

Capital expenditure evaluation—as a means to evaluate anticipated performance from capital expenditures and to provide the mechanism to determine whether projects should be accepted or rejected.

Setting profit goals—by examining internal measurements and external environment, company objectives can be established.

Acquisitions and divestments—used as a means to increase return-on-investment by acquiring or divesting of segments of an organization. The basis for acquiring or divestment can be dictated by return-on-investment objectives.

Product line additions and deletions—will focus on the impact of product profitability for both existing and new products.

Make or buy, lease or purchase—measures the alternatives by comparing return-on-investment impact.

Inventory control—reflects incremental inventory and the impact on earnings from additional inventory.

Pricing—used as a guideline for establishing pricing in keeping with return-on-investment objectives.

Concept

To fully understand the return-on-investment concept, it is important to recognize that ROI is merely a ratio. The numerator represents some expected sum (net earnings, earnings before taxes, etc.) over a period of time. The denominator represents an investment which is needed to achieve the expected earnings. Together, they represent a ratio which is referred to as return-on-investment. The definition of what ROI ratio is used, such as return on equity, return on assets, return on capital employed, etc., depends on what investment base is used. For example, if total assets were used as a base, the ROI ratio would be referred to as return on total assets, but the numerator would have to be defined as to its content, such as before tax or after tax. Therefore, it is important that all concerned understand what is included in both the earnings (numerator) and investment (demoninator) so that consistency in using both historical data, as well as forecasted data, is maintained.

Both the investment base and earnings figures can vary depending on what level of the organization you are measuring, and to whom you are reporting. For example, when reporting to stockholders, they are concerned with the return generated from the interest in equity they have in the business. Therefore, companies use net earnings (after-tax) as a percent of total equity. Corporate financial officers use invested capital which includes equity plus long-term liabilities, since they represent long-term financial commitments to banks, bond-holders, etc. On the other hand, operating managers measure assets for which they are held accountable and that are used to optimize earnings such as inventories, receivables, and fixed assets. This evaluation can be made by using earnings before taxes as opposed to net earnings or any combination thereof.

You can see that many different combinations exist. While these combinations impact differently at various levels of the organization, they should be coordinated so that each level relates to the overall organization objectives. Otherwise, lack of coordinated efforts may result in the organization going in different directions and/or missing objectives. If we accept the premise that return-on-investment is everyone's concern, and that the results occur from participation of all disciplines, then coordinated efforts are a must.

STRATEGIES BETWEEN THE ORGANIZATION AND PROFIT PERFORMANCE

To understand how the organization relates to profit performance, an understanding must exist about the elements. The organization refers to either the total organization, or to such components as divisions, accountability centers, profit centers, revenue centers, expense centers, investment centers, etc. These segments will result in the total performance of the company. Therefore, it is important to understand how the organization operates and how segments contribute to profit performance.

The elements are derived, as well as most financial performance indicators, through the two basic financial statements, namely, the Consolidated Statement of Earnings, and the Consolidated Balance Sheet. However, in certain companies that are highly diversified, data for segments of a company may be difficult to obtain. Many large diversified companies only report segments of financial statements for portions of the business, and these segments can be used to evaluate profit performance over a period of time by consistently using this data.

It is assumed that these financial statements exist, and that some familiarity by the reader also exists. Therefore, the contents need very little explanation. Further analysis in this chapter will be presented to look at how various elements reflect overall performance.

From the following statements, we can look at the components of a key financial measurement performance indicator, i.e., return-on-investment. As previously explained, return-on-investment measures past performance and is also used as a device for developing future goals through definitive plans.

CONSOLIDATED STATEMENT OF EARNINGS

	19X1	% of N.S.	19X2	% of N.S.
Net Sales	$140,000	100.0%	$168,000	100.0%
Operating Expenses				
Cost of sales	84,000	60.0	97,440	58.0
Gross margin	56,000	40.0	70,560	42.0
Depreciation	2,800	2.0	3,300	2.0
Selling expenses	8,400	6.0	9,576	5.7
Administrative expenses	16,800	12.0	21,168	12.6
General expenses	7,000	5.0	7,956	4.7
Operating profit	21,000	15.0	28,560	17.0
Other income	1,400	1.0	2,520	1.5
Income before interest expense and provision for income taxes	22,400	16.0	31,080	18.5
Interest expense	2,100	1.5	2,520	1.5
Income before provisions for income taxes	20,300	14.5	28,560	17.0
Provision for income taxes	9,700	6.9	13,760	8.2
Net earnings	$ 10,600	7.6%	$ 14,800	8.8%

CONSOLIDATED BALANCE SHEET

ASSETS	19X1	% of TOTAL	19X2	% of TOTAL
CURRENT ASSETS				
Cash & marketable securities	$ 22,000	21.0%	$ 20,400	18.1%
Accounts receivable-net	15,400	14.7	20,400	18.1%
Inventories	24,000	22.9	26,400	23.3
Prepaid expenses	600	.4	800	.7
Total current assets	62,000	59.0	68,000	60.2
FIXED ASSETS, AT COST				
Land	5,600	5.3	5,600	5.0
Buildings	35,000	33.3	36,000	31.8
Machinery and equipment	14,400	13.7	15,000	13.3
Office equipment	2,000	1.9	2,400	2.1
	57,000	54.2	59,000	52.2
Less: accumulated depreciation	(19,000)	(18.1)	(19,500)	(17.3)
Net Fixed Assets	38,000	36.1	39,500	34.9
Deferred charges	2,600	2.5	3,000	2.7
Intangibles	2,400	2.4	2,500	2.2
TOTAL ASSETS	$105,000	100.0%	$113,000	100.0%

	19X1	% of TOTAL	19X2	% of TOTAL
LIABILITIES				
CURRENT LIABILITIES				
Accounts payable	$ 15,000	14.3%	$ 18,000	16.0%
Debt due within one year	5,200	5.0	5,000	4.4
Accrued expenses	4,500	4.3	3,600	3.2
Federal income taxes payable	5,300	5.0	7,400	6.5
Total current liabilities	30,000	28.6	34,000	30.1
Debt due after year end-8% notes	26,000	24.7	24,000	21.2
TOTAL LIABILITIES	56,000	53.3	58,000	51.3
SHAREHOLDERS' EQUITY				
Preferred stock—5% Cum.	1,000	1.0	1,000	.9
Common stock	19,800	18.9	19,800	17.5
Capital surplus	6,000	5.7	6,000	5.3
Earnings retained in business	22,200	21.1	28,200	25.0
Total Shareholders' Equity	49,000	46.7	55,000	48.7
TOTAL LIABILITIES AND SHAREHOLDERS' EQUITY	$105,000	100.0%	$113,000	100.0%

COMPONENTS

Three elements derived from these financial statements are net sales, net earnings, and investment. From these elements we can develop the two components of return-on-investment, namely, the profitability rate and the turnover rate. The following illustrates the relationship of these components to the total return-on-investment measurement.

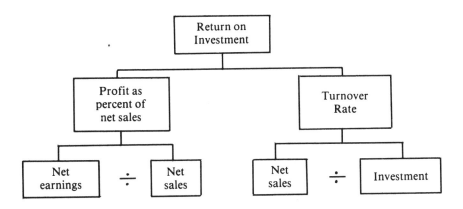

These components, when looked at independently, will answer many questions as to comparative performance. They will also bring to light such questions as:

17

Why was the goal achieved or underachieved?
What areas of the business met or did not meet assigned standards?
What areas of the business need corrective actions?
Where can resources be added or deleted to maximize profits?

PROFITABILITY RATE

The profitability rate measures the profit return for every dollar of sales. It answers the question, for every dollar of sales I make, how much should result in profits? The following illustrates how the profitability rate is calculated. Note that the data for both years came from the earnings statement, and two of the three elements are utilized, namely, net sales and net earnings. The other element, investment, will be utilized in the calculation of turnover.

The profitability rates for years 19X1 and 19X2 are 7.6% and 8.8% respectively. It is possible to analyze why the profitability rate was 1.2 percentage points higher by reviewing the data. The following analysis reflects that increase.

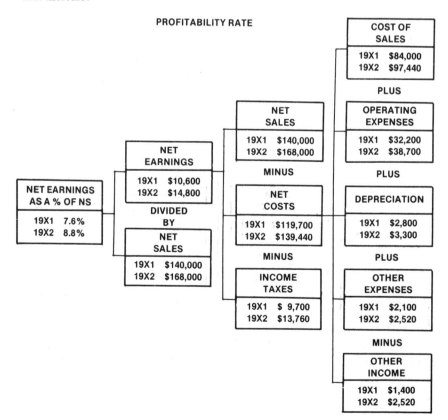

	% of net sales point change
higher gross margin	2.0
lower selling expenses	.3
higher administrative expenses	(.6)
lower general expenses	.3
higher other income	.5
higher income taxes	(1.3)
net increase	1.2

Note: Refer to % of net sales as shown on the comparative
Consolidated Statement of Earnings.

With this type of analysis, it is possible to develop strategies for taking corrective actions. The area needing attention is administrative expenses which are part of operating expenses. Operating expenses increased $19,940 (excluding depreciation) of which $4,368 or 21.9% was due to higher administrative expenses. Gross margin increased 26.0%, consisting of a 20.0% increase in net sales, with only a 16.0% increase in cost of sales. A close look at individual administrative expenses would reveal areas needing attention.

TURNOVER RATE

The turnover rate provides the key to investment turnover, and is used to complete the return-on-investment ratio. Using the data as presented on the

TURNOVER RATE

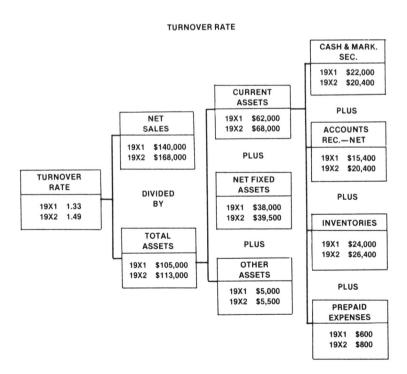

Consolidated Balance Sheet, the following is presented using total assets as the investment base.

The turnover rate only increased marginally by .16 turns due to increased current assets and increased net fixed assets. Further analysis can determine why the various accounts increased such as higher accounts receivable, inventories, and fixed assets. The relationship of these increases in assets is compared to what earnings were generated from the profitability ratio. Together, they form the calculation for return on total assets as follows:

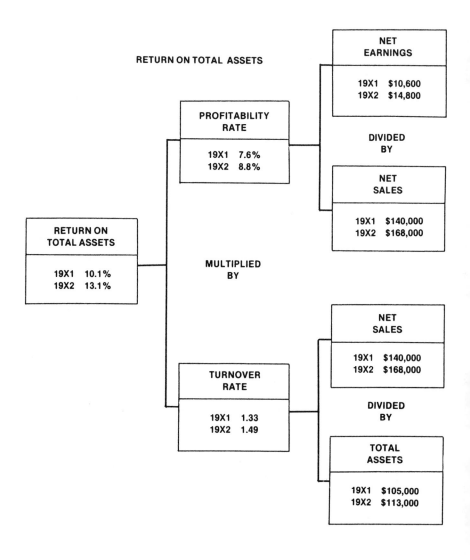

HOW TO INCREASE RETURN
ON TOTAL ASSETS

The return on total assets (ROTA) can be increased in many ways. Certain management decisions will increase profitability. However, it is important to recognize that these decisions are subject to the constraints of the marketplace, corporate philosophy, and the ability to carry out these programs. In addition, where start-up situations occur, as well as new product development, temporary lower returns may occur to provide a base for growth.

While it is recognized that certain decisions would impact on other elements of return on total assets, the following calculations are presented to show the individual impact on one element at a time. This approach dramatizes the significance of sales increases on all and/or selected products, changing sales mix to sell more profitable products, reducing expenses through effective cost control programs, reducing investment through more effective cash management, lowering receivables by more effective credit and collection policies, and reducing obsolete and slow moving inventory. The following management decisions affect return on total assets by either increasing or decreasing both earnings and/or investment.

▢ Increase sales prices (assumption 10%).

	Original Data	Revised Data	Change
Net sales	$168,000	$184,800	$16,800
Net earnings	14,800	16,280	$ 1,480
Total assets	$113,000	$113,000	—
ROTA	13.1%	14.4%	1.3

▢ Reduce operating expenses, such as production, general and administrative costs, and selling costs (assumption 10%).

	Original Data	Revised Data	Change
Net sales	$168,000	$168,000	—
Net earnings	14,800	22,026	$7,226
Total assets	$113,000	$113,000	—
ROTA	13.1%	19.5%	6.4

▢ Reduce current assets such as cash, receivables, and inventories to more desirable levels (assumption 10%).

	Original Data	Revised Data	Change
Net sales	$168,000	$168,000	—
Net earnings	14,800	14,800	—
Total assets	$113,000	$106,200	($6,800)
ROTA	13.1%	13.9%	.8

If all operating decisions were made to bring about all the assumptions, the company would have increased return on total assets from 13.1% to 20.7%, calculated as follows:

	Original Data	Revised Data	Change
Net sales	$168,000	$184,800	$16,800
Net earnings	14,800	22,026	7,226
Total assets	$113,000	$106,200	($6,800)
ROTA	13.1%	20.7%	7.6

ANALYZING ROI VARIANCE

In analyzing the ROI variances, it is necessary to review variances as they relate to both the net earnings (numerator), and total assets (denominator). Since ROI is a function of earnings and investment, both elements must be analyzed to reflect the impact on overall ROI. This is done by keeping one element constant and the other variable. In the case of net earnings variance the investment or total assets is kept constant, and the two comparative figures of net earnings are variable. When analyzing total asset variance, the net earnings are constant and the total assets variable. The following is an analysis of the two comparative years, 19X1 and 19X2, as presented in the previous financial statements.

	19X1	19X2	Variance
Net earnings	$ 10,600	$ 14,800	$4,200
Total assets	$105,000	$113,000	8,000
Return on Total Assets	10.1%	13.1%	3.0

The following analysis will explain the 3.0 percentage point variance between net earnings and total assets.

Net earnings variance

$$\frac{19X2 \text{ net earnings}}{19X1 \text{ total assets}} = \frac{\$ 14,800}{\$105,000} \qquad 14.1\%$$

$$\frac{19X1 \text{ net earnings}}{19X1 \text{ total assets}} = \frac{\$ 10,600}{\$105,000} \qquad 10.1$$

Favorable net earnings variance   4.0

Total asset variance

$$\frac{19X2 \text{ net earnings}}{19X2 \text{ total assets}} = \frac{\$ 14,800}{\$113,000} \qquad 13.1\%$$

$$\frac{19X2 \text{ net earnings}}{19X1 \text{ total assets}} = \frac{\$ 14,800}{\$105,000} \qquad 14.1$$

Unfavorable total asset variance   (1.0)

Net variance   3.0

SUMMARY

You can see how strategies can be developed within the organization resulting in higher ROI performance. Decisions do impact performance, although not as dramatically as presented, but certainly noticeably. Therefore, to improve performance, definable objectives must be established throughout the organization, and measurement techniques must be available to monitor performance. Accomplishing this part of the management process will lead to a more healthy and sound organization.

3

STRATEGIES
BY ANALYSIS

In analyzing any business, it is important that comparative and/or analytical data be provided to measure performance. When reviewing financial reports, historical information is provided, which may or may not provide the necessary information to evaluate current performance. True, comparative years are presented, but it does not always review performance in a way that management can make operating decisions. Therefore, it is important to provide the reader with comparisons that are meaningful.

Performance measurements will provide the internal tools to assist in operating the business, and may also provide important information for the outside community. For example, competitors will continually monitor your performance and use techniques to counteract any competitive edge you may enjoy; the analysts will scrutinize your performance when recommending your company as a sound investment; banks will establish credit lines in accordance with performance both past and future; your customers will review your company as to whether you meet their current demands, and provide the soundness to meet their future needs; and your suppliers will review your performance as to what credit risk they are willing to assume. You can see that analytical data plays an important part in operating the business, both internally and externally.

Comparisons are made over periods of time. They may be daily, weekly, monthly, quarterly, semi-annually, or yearly. Other time periods may be established as the need arises. When comparing within an industry, comparisons can be made as against the total industry, the average of certain segments in the industry, or against key major competitors. When measuring against other than competitors, comparisons can be made on some economic size, i.e., dollar volume, physical size, or asset size.

ANALYZING THE BALANCE SHEET

In analyzing the balance sheet, major segments must be reviewed as follows:

Assets	Liabilities & Shareholders' Equity
Current Assets	Current Liabilities
└────── Net Working Capital ──────┘	
Net fixed assets	Contingent liabilities
Deferred charges	Debt due after one year
Intangibles	Shareholders' equity

The above represents the major segments of the balance sheet, which represents what a company owns and owes to others at a particular point in time. Assets must equal liabilities and shareholders' equity. The assets represent the value of goods and property that is owned, as well as funds on hand and those yet to be received from customers. The liabilities represent all claims due others. Shareholders' equity represents the ownership in the company.

Let's review each major segment and use the following financial statements as previously presented as an example. Analytical ratios, using these statements as a base, will be presented later in this chapter.

Consolidated Balance Sheet
19X2

Assets	
Cash & marketable securities	$ 20,400
Accounts receivable–net	20,400
Inventories	26,400
Prepaid expenses	800
Total current assets	68,000
Fixed assets, at cost	
Land	5,600
Buildings	36,000
Machinery & equipment	15,000
Office equipment	2,400
	59,000
Less: accumulated depreciation	19,500
Net fixed assets	39,500
Deferred charges	3,000
Intangibles	2,500
Total assets	$113,000

Liabilities & Shareholders' Equity
Liabilities
Current liabilities

Accounts payable	$ 18,000
Debt due within one-year	5,000
Accrued expenses	4,500
Federal income taxes payable	6,500
Total current liabilities	34,000
Debt due after one-year	24,000
Total liabilities	58,000
Shareholders' Equity	
Preferred stock	1,000
Common stock	19,800
Capital surplus	6,000
Earnings retained in business	28,200
Total shareholders' equity	55,000
Total liabilities & shareholders' equity	$113,000

Current assets—$68,000. Represents those assets which can be turned into cash in the normal course of business, within one year from the date of the issued balance sheet. They include cash, marketable securities, accounts receivable, inventories, and prepaid expenses.

Current liabilities—$34,000. Includes all obligations that are to be paid, or fall due within the present operating year. Included are accounts payable, debts due within one year, accrued expenses and federal income taxes payable.

Net working capital—$34,000. Represents the difference between current assets and current liabilities.

Net fixed assets—$39,500. Those physical assets that are used in the business to carry out the plans, and are not intended for sale. They include land, buildings, machinery and equipment, and office equipment. With the exception of land, these assets are depreciated which represents declining values of the asset over a specified period of time due to use and/or obsolescence. The gross assets are reduced by accumulated depreciation as of the date of the balance sheet to arrive at a net fixed asset value.

Deferred charges—$3,000. An expenditure for which benefits will be received over future years and expressed over a specified period of time.

Intangibles–$2,500. Non-physical assets having value to a company and expressed over a specific period of time. Most commonly used example is goodwill.

Debt due after one-year–$24,000. Obligations not due in current period, but to be paid at some specified date after the current year.

Shareholders' equity–$55,000. Represents the equity interest that owners have in the business, and computed by taking the difference between total assets and total liabilities. Includes preferred stock, common stock, capital surplus and earnings retained in business. Preferred stock represents shares of the company that have preferential priority over dividends and/or distribution of assets in a liquidation situation. On the other hand, common shareholders do not have preference over dividends or in case of liquidation. Dividends are declared by the directors each period, and are usually dependent upon the earnings of the company. Capital surplus represents the amount over the par or legal value of the stock paid in by the shareholders. Earnings retained in the business are earnings that have been accumulated over time after dividends have been paid to all shareholders.

ANALYZING THE INCOME STATEMENT

This statement represents the results of operating the business and is presented on a periodic basis. Both revenues from the sales of products and expenses to manufacture or acquire those products sold, costs of selling and distributing the products, and other costs of operating the business are shown. The result of revenues exceeding costs results in a profit to the company. The following major segments are presented:

Net sales
Cost of sales   **Gross margin**
Depreciation   **Operating profit**
Selling expenses
Administrative expenses   **Operating expenses**
General expenses
Operating profit
Other income/expense   **Net earnings**
Provision for income taxes

You can see how each item of the earnings statement helps to produce a major segment such as gross margin, operating expenses, operating profit, and net earnings. These segments are indicative of how well the company is operating, and the extent to which the business is capable of providing profits for both survival and expansion. The ability to manage the expenses in relationship to revenues produced is a prime function of management. The following Consolidated Statement of Earnings is presented. Analytical ratios will be presented later in the chapter.

Consolidated Statement of Earnings
19X2

Net sales	$168,000
Operating expenses	
Cost of sales	97,440
Gross margin	70,560
Depreciation	3,300
Selling expenses	9,576
Administrative expenses	21,168
General expenses	7,956
Operating profit	28,560
Other income	2,520
Income before interest expense and provision for income taxes	31,080
Interest expense	2,520
Income before provision for income taxes	28,560
Provision for income taxes	13,760
Net earnings	$ 14,800

In reviewing the earnings statement, the reader should analyze the profitability of the company many different ways. How do revenues compare to budget or last year? Are product costs in line with agreed upon standards? What impact did accounting changes have on earnings? Are general and administrative costs in line? Is it costing more to sell a product than planned, and if so, should prices be increased to absorb those rising costs? These are just a few of the questions that can be raised when reviewing performance from the earnings statement.

RATIOS

To assist in analyzing the peformance of a company and/or its operations, it is important to understand financial ratios and how they are used. Ratios are used to show relationships between sets of data as well as trends, and lead to possible corrective actions that may be necessary to carry out the objectives of the company.

These financial ratios are derived from the balance sheet and the statement of earnings. They are used as measurements of management performance, versus checkpoints of other companies. They can be developed at various levels of activity within a company. Most activities of a company have some impact on financial statements, therefore financial ratios can be developed to follow along organizational lines. At various levels of the organization different management criteria are selected. For example, the higher the level of responsibility in the organization, the more interest in the overall performance of the company and the impact on external environment. The lower the level of responsibility, the more concern with day-to-day operations. Regardless of priorities and responsibilities, total objectives of the company remain the same.

As indicated, ratio activity can be reviewed at different levels within the organization. At each level different types of ratios are reviewed. They will be referred to as performance ratios, managing ratios, and profitability ratios. While they represent only guidelines in providing facts for interpretation, they are a vital tool in operating the business. The following are examples of these three types of ratio activity that a manager can review.

Performance ratios. Review the overall performance of a company, and are viewed by the outside community as a means of measuring current and potential performance.

Net earnings to shareholders' equity—represents the rate of earnings on owners' capital that is invested in the business.

$$\frac{\text{net earnings}}{\text{shareholders' equity}} = \frac{\$14,800}{\$55,000} = 26.9\%$$

Net earnings to total assets—represents the rate of return on all funds invested in the business by both owners and creditors, and measures use of capacity and operating efficiency.

$$\frac{\text{net earnings}}{\text{total assets}} = \frac{\$14,800}{\$113,000} = 13.1\%$$

Net earnings per common share—indicates the per share return to common shareholders.

$$\frac{\text{net earnings}}{\begin{array}{c}\text{number of common}\\\text{shares outstanding}\end{array}} = \frac{\$14,800}{\$6,600} = \$2.24 \text{ per share}$$

Market price of stock to net earnings per share—commonly referred to as the price-earning ratio. It is a reflection of investor confidence.

$$\frac{\text{market price per share}}{\text{earnings per share}} = \frac{\$33.00}{\$2.24} = 14.7 \text{ times}$$

Payout ratio—measures the amount of dividends paid from net earnings and the amount reinvested in the business.

$$\frac{\text{dividends}}{\text{net earnings}} = \frac{\$8,800}{\$14,800} = 59.5\%$$

Net earnings to tangible net worth—indicates the ability to provide dividends and/or provide future growth from net earnings.

$$\frac{\text{net worth}}{\text{tangible net worth}} = \frac{\$14,800}{\$52,500} = 28.2\%$$

Net sales to tangible net worth—indicates the turnover of invested capital.

$$\frac{\text{net earnings}}{\text{tangible net worth}} = \frac{\$168,000}{\$52,500} = 3.2 \text{ times}$$

Managing ratios. Evaluate the various items of the balance sheet, and are used to manage such major areas of the company as cash, inventories, receivables, and debt relationships.

Current ratio—a general indication of the ability of the company to meet its current obligations.

$$\frac{\text{total current assets}}{\text{total current liabilities}} = \frac{\$68,000}{\$34,000} = 2.0 \text{ times}$$

Acid test—an indication of the ability of the company to meet current obligations by placing emphasis on those liquid assets which can be quickly converted into cash.

$$\frac{\text{quick assets*}}{\text{total current liabilities}} = \frac{\$40,800}{\$34,000} = 1.2 \text{ times}$$

*includes cash, marketable securities, and receivables.

Debt to equity—the extent to which a company is financed by borrowed capital, and the extent to which a company is financed by permanent contributed capital. A measurement often referred to by lending institutions.

$$\frac{\text{shareholders' equity}}{\text{debt due after one-year}} = \frac{\$55,000}{\$24,000} = 2.3 \text{ times}$$

Net sales to accounts receivable—indicates the turnover of receivables during the year.

$$\frac{\text{net sales}}{\text{accounts receivable}} = \frac{\$168,000}{\$20,400} = 8.2 \text{ times}$$

Days sales outstanding—indicates the average age of accounts receivable, and control over collections.

$$\frac{\text{accounts receivable}}{\text{average daily sales*}} = \frac{\$20,400}{\$460.27} = 44.3 \text{ days sales outstanding}$$
*net sales divided by 365

Inventory turnover—highlights possible excessive inventory by analyzing turnover.

$$\frac{\text{cost of sales}}{\text{inventories}} = \frac{\$97,440}{\$26,400} = 3.7 \text{ times}$$

Days sales on hand—indicates the average length of time that inventory is held before sale.

$$\frac{\text{inventories}}{\text{average daily cost of sales*}} = \frac{\$26,400}{\$266.96} = 98.9 \text{ days sales on hand}$$
*cost of sales divided by 365

Working capital turnover—indicates the activity of working capital and its utilization.

$$\frac{\text{net sales}}{\text{working capital}} = \frac{\$168,000}{\$34,000} = 4.9 \text{ times}$$

Liquidity ratio—indicates the ability of a company to convert assets into cash promptly to meet short-term obligations.

$$\frac{\text{cash \& marketable securities}}{\text{total current liabilities}} = \frac{\$20,400}{\$34,000} = 60.0\%$$

Days sales in total current liabilities—indicates the number of days sales needed to meet total current liabilities.

$$\frac{\text{total current liabilities}}{\text{average daily sales*}} = \frac{\$34,000}{\$460.27} = 73.9 \text{ days}$$
*net sales divided by 365

Net earnings to working capital—indicates the ability to meet fund requirements for day-to-day operations.

$$\frac{\text{net earnings}}{\text{working capital}} = \frac{\$14,800}{\$34,000} = 43.5\%$$

Net sales to inventories—indicates a measurement for comparing inventories in stock to sales.

$$\frac{\text{net sales}}{\text{inventories}} = \frac{\$168,000}{\$26,400} = 6.4 \text{ times}$$

Net fixed assets to tangible net worth—indicates the extent to which tangible investment by the owners is tied up in net fixed assets.

$$\frac{\text{net fixed assets}}{\text{tangible net worth}} = \frac{\$39,500}{\$52,500} = 75.2\%$$

Debt due after one-year to working capital—indicates the contribution by long-term creditors to the working funds of the company.

$$\frac{\text{debt due after one-year}}{\text{working capital}} = \frac{\$24,000}{\$34,000} = 70.6\%$$

Shareholders' equity to total assets—indicates the amount of total resources obtained from owner's contribution.

$$\frac{\text{shareholders' equity}}{\text{total assets}} = \frac{\$55,000}{\$113,000} = 48.7\%$$

Current liabilities to tangible net worth—indicates the degree of equity protection provided by the owners to the short-term creditors.

$$\frac{\text{current liabilities}}{\text{tangible net worth}} = \frac{\$34,000}{\$52,500} = 64.8\%$$

Total debt to tangible net worth—indicates the amount of equity the creditors have in the assets in relation to the owners.

$$\frac{\text{total debt}}{\text{tangible net worth}} = \frac{\$29,000}{\$52,500} = 55.2\%$$

Inventories to working capital—indicates the relationship of inventory balances to working capital, or the portion of working capital represented by inventories.

$$\frac{\text{inventories}}{\text{working capital}} = \frac{\$26,400}{\$34,000} = 77.6\%$$

Debt due within one-year to inventories—indicates the extent to which a company relies on funds from selling inventories on hand to meet its debts.

$$\frac{\text{debt due within one-year}}{\text{inventories}} = \frac{\$5,000}{\$26,400} = 18.9\%$$

Profitability ratios.   Relate to the statement of earnings and evaluate the operations of each area of accountability and/or profitability center.
Gross margin to net sales—indicates the percentage margin of sales over the cost of sales.

$$\frac{\text{gross margin}}{\text{net sales}} = \frac{\$70,560}{\$168,000} = 42.0\%$$

Net earnings to net sales—indicates the profitability of sales.

$$\frac{\text{net earnings}}{\text{net sales}} = \frac{\$14,800}{\$168,000} = 8.8\%$$

Selling expenses to net sales—indicates the portion of the sales dollars spent in selling the product.

$$\frac{\text{selling expenses}}{\text{net sales}} = \frac{\$9,576}{\$168,000} = 5.7\%$$

Income before interest expense and provision for income taxes to interest expense—indicates the ability of a company to meet interest costs through borrowed funds.

$$\frac{\text{income before interest expense and provision for income taxes}}{\text{interest expense}} = \frac{\$31,080}{\$2,520} = 12.3 \text{ times}$$

Operating expenses to net sales—indicates a measurement of operating efficiency.

$$\frac{\text{operating expenses}}{\text{net sales}} = \frac{\$139,400}{\$168,000} = 83.0\%$$

Financial Ratio Matrix

In looking at the summation of the ratios just presented, it is possible to develop a financial ratio matrix, which would reflect the various impacts on both the balance sheet and earnings statement. You will note that each of the major types of ratios impact different segments of these statements. Different segments are used in various parts of the organization for analyzing and controlling the business. It is, therefore, possible to establish ratio objectives at each operating level of the organization and assign accountability. In total, the matrix is utilized to achieve over-all performance, while establishing operating control at each level. The following reflects the previously discussed ratios. Additonal ratios may also be used to further support the financial activity of a company. The need to analyze and control other organizational segments should be reviewed and developed accordingly. The importance in your business of each ratio will determine the matrix that you will finally develop.

BALANCE SHEET

CM	CASH AND MARKETABLE SECURITIES
QA	QUICK ASSETS
AR	ACCOUNTS RECEIVABLE
INV	INVENTORIES
CA	CURRENT ASSETS
CL	CURRENT LIABILITIES
NFA	NET FIXED ASSETS
TA	TOTAL ASSETS
WC	WORKING CAPITAL
LTD	DEBT DUE AFTER ONE-YEAR
TNW	TANGIBLE NET WORTH
SE	SHAREHOLDERS' EQUITY
TD	TOTAL DEBT
STD	DEBT DUE WITHIN ONE-YEAR
DIV	DIVIDENDS
CS	COMMON SHARES OUTSTANDING
MP	MARKET PRICE PER SHARE
EPS	EARNINGS PER SHARE

STATEMENT OF EARNINGS

GM	GROSS MARGIN
NS	NET SALES
NE	NET EARNINGS
SEL	SELLING EXPENSES

FINANCIAL RATIO MATRIX

TYPES OF RATIOS	BALANCE SHEET SEGMENTS															EARNINGS SEGMENTS							
	CM	QA	AR	INV	CA	NFA	TA	CL	STD	WC	LTD	TD	TNW	SE	DIV	NS	CS	GM	OE	SEL	IBI	IE	NE
PERFORMANCE																							
NE/SE																							X
NE/TA							X																X
NE/CS																							X
MP/EPS														X									X
DW/NE															X								X
NE/TNW													X										X
NS/TNW													X			X							-
MANAGING																							
CA/CL					X			X															
QA/CL		X						X															
SE/LTD											X			X									
NS/AR			X													X							
AR/ADS			X													X							
CS/INV				X													X						
INV/ADC				X													X						
NS/WC										X						X							
CM/CL	X							X								X							
CL/ADS								X								X							
CA/STD					X				X														
NE/WC										X						X							
NS/INV				X												X							
NFA/TNW						X							X										
LTD/WC										X	X												
SE/TA							X							X									
CL/TNW								X					X										
TD/TNW												X	X										
INV/WC				X						X													
STD/INV				X					X														
PROFITABILITY																							
GM/NS																X		X					
NE/NS																X							X
SEL/NS																X				X			
IBI/IE																					X	X	
OE/NS																X			X				

35

IBI	INCOME BEFORE INTEREST EXPENSE AND PROVISION FOR INCOME TAXES
IE	INTEREST EXPENSE
OE	OPERATING EXPENSES
CS	COST OF SALES
ADS	AVERAGE DAILY SALES
ADC	AVERAGE DAILY COST OF SALES

SUMMARY

In summary, ratios develop relationships between items, as recorded on both the balance sheet and earnings statement. Since they reflect both financial statements, the possibility of developing hundreds of ratios exists. These ratios give you some clues as to what is happening in the organization, and at what levels. This is a technique of developing trends, and is based on past performance. The use of ratios should not be considered as a forecasting tool, but merely for guidelines in putting into perspective, facts for the interpretation and further analysis of the financial picture. Caution should be given to understand and recognize accounting conventions and changes produced so as to not arrive at erroneous conclusions. The recognition that financial ratios are only one tool of measuring performance will enable an organization to integrate this tool with other evaluative tools for better performance. Remember, ratios represent the combination of recorded transactions, accounting conventions, and operating skills. Therefore it must be recognized that depending on financial ratios requires caution.

SOURCE AND APPLICATION
OF FUNDS STRATEGY

The source and application of funds statement indicates the flow of money through the business by highlighting where cash was used and where cash was spent. Cash in this statement also refers to certain non-cash items, such as depreciation. Since no actual payment of cash is made, it does free additional funds through savings on taxes, and is considered a source of funds. See discussion on cash flow and depreciation.

CONCEPT

The concept of source and application of funds is found in certain basic principles as follows:

A source of funds decreases assets, increases liabilities and net worth, and includes net earnings and non-cash charges, such as depreciation as reflected in the earnings statement. An application of funds increases assets and decreases liabilities and net worth.

With this basic principle, any year's activity can be computed by merely comparing the changes in balance sheet accounts and reflecting those items in the current year's earnings statement, namely, net earnings and non-cash charges.

The effect of cash flow is a vital element to the success of the business. More companies evidence financial problems through poor utilization of cash than any other factor in the financial statements. The source and application of funds statement reflects those changes by showing how cash is increased and decreased through management decisions, and the result of those decisions on the entire business.

Decisions That Increase Cash

Many decisions reflect increases in cash. It is obvious that it is important to the survival of the business and emphasis should be placed on those decisions that increase cash. They are as follows:

Lower accounts receivables due to declines in unit and/or dollar volume, shorter terms of sale, and faster collections.

Selling off of non-salable merchandise.

Liquidation of unproductive fixed assets and investments.

Deferred and prepaid expense decreases.

Deferred or nonpayment liability increases.

Short and long-term borrowings.

New equity capital.

Earnings retained in the business.

Non-cash charges, such as depreciation.

While these decisions increase cash, they also may generate other decisions that decrease cash.

Decisions That Decrease Cash

Higher accounts receivables due to higher unit and/or dollar volume, longer sales terms, and slower collections.

Build-ups of inventory.

Investment and fixed asset acquisitions.

Deferred and prepaid expense increases.

Payments made for taxes, dividends, research and development, and any other operational expenditures not included in the above decisions.

Short and long-term prepayment of borrowings.

Equity capital retirements.

Losses in operations.

As you can see, most operational decisions reflect cash in some way. The results of those decisions are shown in the following statement.

Source and Application of Funds

Total Assets	19X1	19X2	Increase or (Decrease)	Source or (Application)
Current assets				
Cash and marketable securities	$ 22,000	$ 20,400	($1,600)	Source
Accounts receivable—net	15,400	20,400	5,000	Application
Inventories	24,000	26,400	2,400	Application
Prepaid expenses	600	800	200	Application
Total current assets	62,000	68,000	6,000	—
Fixed assets				
Land	5,600	5,600	—	—
Buildings	35,000	36,000	1,000	Application
Machinery and equipment	14,400	15,000	600	Application
Office equipment	2,000	2,400	400	Application
	57,000	59,000	2,000	—
Less: accumulated depreciation	16,200	19,500	3,300	Source
Net fixed assets	40,800	39,500	(1,300)	—
Deferred charges	200	3,000	2,800	Application
Intangibles	2,000	2,500	500	Application
Total assets	$105,000	$113,000	$8,000	—
Total Liabilities & Net Worth				
Current liabilities				
Accounts payable	$ 15,000	$ 18,000	$3,000	Source
Debt due within one-year	5,200	5,000	(200)	Application
Accrued expenses	4,000	4,500	500	Source
Federal income taxes payable	5,800	6,500	700	Source
Total current liabilities	30,000	34,000	4,000	—
Debt due after one-year	26,000	24,000	(2,000)	Application
Preferred stock	1,000	1,000	—	—
Common stock	19,800	19,800	—	—
Capital surplus	6,000	6,000	—	—
Earnings retained in business	22,200	28,200	6,000	Source
Total liabilities and net worth	$105,000	$113,000	$8,000	—

Note that increases or decreases in the balance sheet accounts are reflected between years 19X1 and 19X2. The objective is to show the changes from the two periods and classify those changes as to a source or application of funds in accordance with the concept as outlined previously. Two significant items need to be explored. They are accumulated depreciation and earnings retained in the business.

Accumulated depreciation represents the depreciation accumulated as of the date of the balance sheet. For purposes of source and application of funds, depreciation expense is used as reflected in the earnings statement. In this example the amounts are similar, but in actual practice, they would differ.

The other item is earnings retained in the business, and represents the balance at year-end reflecting net earnings or net losses of operations, less payments paid to stockholders as dividends, and any other change resulting in monies accumulated which are retained in the business. The following Accumulated Retained Earnings Statement reflects the increase of $6,000 in the retained earnings account as shown on the source and application of funds statement. The additions to cash are net earnings and the decreases of cash are dividends paid to both preferred and common stockholders.

Accumulated Retained Earnings Statement

	19X2
Balance at beginning of year	$22,200
Net earnings for the year	14,800
Total	37,000
Less: dividends paid on:	
preferred stock	500
common stock	8,300
Balance at end of year	$28,200

SOURCE AND APPLICATION OF FUNDS STATEMENT

The following statement summarizes both items of source and application of funds. The changes must equal each other or be in balance, indicating that all items have been accounted for properly. Note that it is the one financial statement that reflects operational results in both the Earnings Statement and the Balance Sheet.

Source and Application of Funds

	Source of Funds	Application of Funds
Net earnings	$14,800	
Depreciation expense	3,300	
Decrease in assets		
Cash and marketable securities	1,600	
Increase in liabilities and net worth		
Accounts payable	3,000	
Accrued expenses	500	
Federal income taxes payable	700	

Debt due within one-year		$ 200
Debt due after one-year		2,000
Dividends paid-preferred stock		500
Dividends paid-common stock		8,300
Increase in assets		
Accounts receivable-net		5,000
Inventories		2,400
Prepaid expenses		200
Buildings-Gross		1,000
Machinery and equipment-Gross		600
Office equipment-Gross		400
Deferred charges		2,800
Intangibles		500
Total	$23,900	$23,900

Another way of reviewing the source and application of funds is to establish the change in cash and marketable securities from period to period, in this case a reduction of $1,600 ($22,000-$20,400), and determine what factors caused the change in this balance. The following statement shows this approach.

CHANGE IN CASH AND MARKETABLE SECURITIES

Balance at beginning of year	$22,000
SOURCE OF FUNDS	
Net earnings	14,800
Depreciation expense	3,300
Total available funds	40,100

APPLICATION OF FUNDS

Accounts payable	(3,000)
Accrued expenses	(500)
Federal income taxes payable	(700)
Debt due within one-year	200
Debt due after one-year	2,000
Dividends paid	8,800
Accounts receivable-net	5,000
Inventories	2,400
Prepaid expenses	200
Fixed assets-gross	2,000
Deferred charges	2,800
Intangibles	500
Balance at end of year	$20,400

It is now evident why the cash and marketable securities balance declined from 19X1 to 19X2. Major items accounting for this reduction were dividends paid ($8,800), higher accounts receivable-net ($5,000), additions to fixed assets ($2,000), higher inventories ($2,400) and higher deferred charges ($2,800). This was partially offset by higher accounts payable ($3,000), accrued expenses ($500), and federal income taxes payable ($700).

Changes in Working Capital

One important element resulting from this analysis is the change in working capital. Defined as current assets less current liabilities, it reflects the ability of a company to meet its current obligations, or how many dollars of current assets are available to pay creditors if liquidation were necessary. In the preceding example, working capital changed as follows:

CHANGES IN CURRENT ASSETS

Cash and marketable securities	($1,600)
Accounts receivable-net	5,000
Inventories	2,400
Prepaid expenses	200
Total	$6,000

CHANGES IN CURRENT LIABILITIES

Accounts payable	$3,000
Debt due within one-year	(200)
Accrued expenses	500
Federal income taxes payable	700
Total	$4,000

WORKING CAPITAL

Balance at beginning of year	$32,000
Add increases in current assets	6,000
Deduct increases in current liabilites	(4,000)
Balance at end of year	$34,000

Working Capital Ratios

These ratios will serve as an indicator in appraising the working capital condition of the company. The relationship should be measured as it relates to historical trends, internal trends, competitive trends, and the requirements of the company.

Current ratio. Provides a general indication of the ability of a company to meet its current obligations.

$$\frac{\text{Current assets}}{\text{Current liabilities}} = \overset{\text{19X1}}{\frac{\$62,000}{\$30,000}} = 2.1 \text{ times} \quad \overset{\text{19X2}}{\frac{\$68,000}{\$34,000}} = 2.0 \text{ times}$$

Quick ratio (acid test). An indication of the ability of a company to meet current obligations by placing emphasis on those liquid assets which can be quickly converted into cash.

$$\frac{\text{Cash \& marketable securities and receivables}}{\text{Current liabilities}} = \overset{\text{19X1}}{\frac{\$37,400}{\$30,000}} = 1.2 \text{ times} \quad \overset{\text{19X2}}{\frac{\$40,800}{\$34,000}} = 1.2 \text{ times}$$

Inventories to working capital. Measures the impact of inventories on liquidity.

$$\frac{\text{Inventories}}{\text{Working capital}} = \overset{\text{19X1}}{\frac{\$24,000}{\$32,000}} = 75.0\% \quad \overset{\text{19X2}}{\frac{\$26,400}{\$34,000}} = 77.6\%$$

Accounts receivable-net to working capital. Measures the impact of accounts receivable-net on liquidity.

$$\frac{\text{Accounts receivable-net}}{\text{Working capital}} = \overset{\text{19X1}}{\frac{\$15,400}{\$32,000}} = 48.1\% \quad \overset{\text{19X2}}{\frac{\$20,400}{\$34,000}} = 60.0\%$$

Net earnings to working capital. Ability of a company to use working capital to generate net earnings.

$$\frac{\text{Net earnings}}{\text{Working capital}} = \overset{\text{19X1}}{\frac{\$10,600}{\$32,000}} = 33.1\% \quad \overset{\text{19X2}}{\frac{\$14,800}{\$34,000}} = 43.5\%$$

Net sales to accounts receivable-net. Reflects the turnover of receivables. Higher ratios indicate the probability of faster collection of sales.

$$\frac{\text{Net sales}}{\text{Accounts receivable-net}} = \overset{\text{19X1}}{\frac{\$140,000}{\$15,400}} = 9.1 \text{ times} \overset{\text{19X2}}{\frac{\$168,000}{\$20,400}} = 8.2 \text{ times}$$

Cost of sales to inventories. Shows the turnover of inventories. Lower ratios indicate the possibility of excessive inventory and/or obsolete merchandise.

$$\frac{\text{Cost of sales}}{\text{Inventories}} = \overset{\text{19X1}}{\frac{\$84,000}{\$24,000}} = 3.5 \text{ times} \overset{\text{19X2}}{\frac{\$97,440}{\$26,400}} = 3.7 \text{ times}$$

Net sales to working capital. Indicates working capital turnover.

$$\frac{\text{Net sales}}{\text{Working capital}} = \overset{\text{19X1}}{\frac{\$140,000}{\$32,000}} = 4.4 \text{ times} \overset{\text{19X2}}{\frac{\$168,000}{\$34,000}} = 4.9 \text{ times}$$

In summarizing the ratios affecting working capital, trends are developed between 19X1 and 19X2 that must be reviewed to develop operational objectives. Putting these ratios in perspective as to past performance and industry performance will serve as a barometer for future performance.

	Summary of Working Capital Ratios	
	19X1	19X2
Current ratio	2.1 times	2.0 times
Quick ratio	1.2 times	1.2 times
Inventories to working capital	75.0%	77.6%
Accounts receivable-net to working capital	48.1%	60.0%
Net earnings to working capital	33.1%	43.5%
Net sales to accounts receivable-net	9.1 times	8.2 times
Cost of sales to inventories	3.5 times	3.7 times
Net sales to working capital	4.4 times	4.9 times

The above ratios can be analyzed by reviewing the source and application of funds statement. The changes in working capital accounts will explain the changes in working capital ratios.

We just reviewed how operational decisions can impact on working capital as well as ratio performance. Its ultimate effect is on return-on-investment. The following calculation using funds employed (total assets less current liabilities) as an investment base is presented.

$$\text{Return on funds employed} = \frac{\text{Net earnings}}{\text{Funds employed}}$$

19X1	19X2
$\frac{\$10,600}{\$75,000} = 14.1\%$	$\frac{\$14,800}{\$79,000} = 18.7\%$

If we were to look at return on funds employed for both years, you will note a higher return for 19X2 through greater utilization of funds employed in producing higher net earnings. In proportion, it took fewer funds employed to generate higher net earnings. Net earnings increased 39.6% from 19X1 to 19X2, while funds employed for the same period increased 5.3%. In summary, operational decisions will impact on working capital, and ultimately, return-on-investment.

5

COST DECISIONS AND GROSS MARGIN STRATEGIES

In any business, whether it's selling a product or a service business, it is vital to know all the costs in operating that enterprise. Not only does it reflect earnings, it is also necessary in assigning responsibility for these costs and the ability to generate income over and above those costs. It also generates the mechanism to account for costs so that performance measurement can be attained.

There are many different types of costs which react in various ways. Some costs vary with the volume of the business, while other costs are not dependent on volume; some relate to product or cost centers; some have no implication on long-term behavior; some costs are fully absorbed in the product costs; while others reflect only costs directly attributable to the product. You can see that costing is not an easy exercise, but does provide some thought and direction as to its use in measuring performance. These costs will be briefly explored later in the chapter.

In order for the business as a whole to be profitable and survive, each segment must provide some economic worth, or at the very least, be minimally profitable. Or to put it in other terms, to be unprofitable in the long-run is to be unsound economically. Therefore, segments of the business (see chapter 1) must be categorized and evaluated as follows:

By total business—must be profitable or provide income over and above expenses to enhance growth and/or generate funds to committed programs of activity.

By division—must provide funds needed to carry out overall business objectives.

By responsibility or cost center—must provide justification as to contribution to the company, whether in goods or services.

By customer—most customers must be at least minimally profitable, or provide some economic worth to the business.

By product—similar to by customer.

Others—measured in terms of risk and contribution to the business.

Many measurement tools can be used as explained in later chapters. Whatever the tool used, it must provide the basis for evaluating performance, and provide management with operating decisions to enhance growth, or at the very least, maintain current levels of performance.

COST DEFINITIONS

As previously indicated, costs can be defined many ways depending upon the nature of the evaluating system. They can be used in different ways, and can have impact on management decisions, e.g., direct vs. absorption costing. Since costs are expenditures for some economic benefit, they are generally expected to support and/or generate revenues for the business. These benefits may be received at the time the expenditure is made, before the expenditure had been made, or at some future date. The classification of how the cost is accounted for is dependent upon when the benefits were derived.

Management's effectiveness is greatly enhanced by being able to account for and identify cost data. It is a mechanism that establishes controls over expenditures and sets in motion one of management's basic responsibilities, that of planning business decisions to efficiently and economically manage the business to produce an economic worth. In addition, decisions can be reached as to how resources and effort can be allocated in establishing objectives for both current and future earnings. This is accomplished by measuring the effectiveness of cost data with past performance, and the effect of possible alternative actions.

Costs are affected in many ways by many activities both internally and externally. They are affected by the rate of activity that is generated by changes in sales and production volume. The way management operates the business is affected in another way. This will create cost changes by influences of management's attitudes, and the effect of introducing new changes, or new ways of operating the business. With these internal influences, the external environment will impact significantly on costs. Costs will respond to competitive pressures, economic environment, technology, political environment, as well as the social environment.

These actions are based on measuring expected or budgeted costs with actual costs incurred. These decision alternatives are one of a manager's objectives in identifying those costs which are controllable, and associating those costs with decision alternatives such as pricing, product mix, acquisitions of fixed assets, business segment profitability, inventory evaluation, make or buy decisions, lease or own decisions, and job performance. These are but some of the decisions that can be reached through identifying costs. It is as stated, the economic benefits that are expected to derive from cost expenditures. To understand cost behavior, it is important to review some of the more commonly used terminology in defining cost classifications. While many more exist, an appreciation will be presented to understand the behavior and/or impact of costs, and the relationship of the decision-making process.

There are two basic types of costs, that is, actual and standard. Actual costs are self-explanatory and include both acquistion and historical costs. Standard costs are anticipated or predetermined costs of producing a unit of output. There are two methods for accumulating costs—job order and process costing. Job order costing accumulates costs of an identifiable product known as a job, and follows the product through the production stages. On the other hand, process costing accumulates costs by a process or operation as it flows through production.

The two widely used approaches are direct and absorption costing. Direct costing only allocates variable costs to the product such as direct materials, direct labor, and direct manufacturing overhead. Fixed costs are treated as period expenses, that is, charged to the period in which they were incurred rather than to the product. In contrast, absorption costing includes manufacturing costs, both variable and fixed, to all units produced. It is commonly referred to as full costing.

While much discussion generates from using direct vs. absorption costing, the use of direct costing for internal reporting will:

assist in product decisions relative to sales mix, as well as marketing decisions.

determine differences between fixed and variable costs in manufacturing, selling, and general and administrative costs.

avoid the need to establish any basis for allocation of fixed expenses, and thus eliminate laborious expense allocations.

establish responsibility reporting based on controllable cost data.

One caution must be recognized, particularly in the areas of pricing. Since not all costs are charged to the product, the possibility exists that management may use this data incorrectly in pricing. An under pricing situation may exist, since direct costing accounts for only direct costs, and may understate the product cost and inflate product margins. Thus, erroneous decisions may develop. The following example illustrates this point.

Product A

	Projected Prices		
	$5.00	**$6.00**	**$7.00**
Projected unit sales	20,000	16,000	12,000
Projected sales dollars	$100,000	$96,000	$84,000
Absorption costing			
Manufacturing cost—			
at $3.00 per unit	60,000	48,000	36,000
Direct costing			
Manufacturing cost—			
at $1.50 per unit	30,000	24,000	18,000
Variable selling cost—			
6% of sales dollars	6,000	5,760	5,040
Gross Margins			
Absorption costing	40,000	48,000	48,000
% of sales dollars	40.0%	50.0%	57.1%
Direct costing	$64,000	$66,240	$60,960
% of sales dollars	64.0%	69.0%	72.6%

You can see that gross margin % varies between absorption and direct costing within each projected price. At the $7.00 price, the percents are 57.1% and 72.6% respectively. It is well to keep in mind that while these percents differ depending upon the method used, they will relate to each other by using one method consistently. The key is to measure these percents using historical data under one method only. Changing methods for comparison or planning purposes will lead to incorrect decisions.

The two costs that relate to products are product costs and period costs. A product cost is any manufacturing cost relating to the product, and relates to revenue in the period in which the product was sold. These costs are part of the inventory value before the sale of the product. On the other hand, period costs are based on periods of time, as opposed to units of a product, and expire with time. These costs are charged against revenue in the period in which the expense was incurred.

Costs that fluctuate directly with volume changes are referred to as variable costs. Those costs that are not directly related to rate of output are called fixed costs. Other types of costs are opportunity costs which represent a benefit that is foregone as a result of not using another alternative, and out-of-pocket costs which are costs that require cash outlays currently, or in the future. A closer look at the impact of absorption costing vs. direct costing is necessary to see how costs are used in management decisions, and as a tool for costing decisions in impacting earnings.

Absorption Costing

The following illustration is an operating statement showing three products, and the costs allocated under absorption costing.

ABSORPTION COSTING
19X2

| | P R O D U C T | | | |
	A	B	C	Total
Net sales	$32,000	$95,000	$41,000	$168,000
Operating Expenses				
Cost of Sales	19,200	53,840	24,400	97,440
Gross margin	12,800	41,160	16,600	70,560
% of Net sales	40.0%	43.3%	40.5%	42.0%
Depreciation	600	1,800	900	3,300
Selling Expenses	1,820	5,410	2,346	9,576
Administrative Expenses	4,000	11,968	5,200	21,168
General Expenses	1,500	4,500	1,956	7,956
TOTAL	7,920	23,678	10,402	42,000
Operating Profit	$ 4,880	$17,482	$ 6,198	$ 28,560
% of Net sales	15.3%	18.4%	15.1%	17.0%

Note that no effort is made to identify fixed vs. variable expenses in both manufacturing costs (costs of sales) as well as selling, administrative and general expenses. In addition, costs are considered as part of the product, not period costs. Also, the manufacturing overhead costs are not reflected in the operating statement until the product is sold, since the costs are still part of the cost of inventory. Using this method does present problems in understanding the behavior of costs, and also makes it difficult to simulate the impact on profits of various alternatives in the planning process.

Direct Costing

Under direct costing only costs identifiable with a product are considered as a cost of that product. To accomplish this and understand cost behavior, costs must be divided into variable and fixed in an effort to develop a product contribution for each product. The following illustrates an operating statement using direct costing.

Note that costs are identified by product, and charged to the period of time in which they were incurred, as opposed to the product. Using this method, earnings are more directly related to sales.

As stated earlier, profits by product will vary due to the timing of when

DIRECT COSTING
19X2

	A	B	C	TOTAL
Net sales	$32,000	$95,000	$41,000	$168,000
Variable Cost of Sales				
Manufacturing	16,600	51,200	18,200	86,000
Selling	1,000	2,600	1,400	5,000
Total	17,600	53,800	19,600	91,000
Variable Contribution	14,400	41,200	21,400	77,000
% of Net Sales	45.0%	43.4%	52.2%	45.8%
Direct Fixed Expenses	700	1,400	900	3,000
Product Contribution	$13,700	$39,800	$20,500	$ 74,000
% of Net Sales	42.8%	41.9%	50.0%	44.0%
Indirect Fixed Expenses				
Manufacturing				14,740
Selling				1,576
Administrative				21,168
General				7,956
Total				45,440
Operating Income				$ 28,560
% of Net Sales				17.0%

the fixed factory overhead is charged to the operating statement. In the case of absorption costing, this expense is charged to inventory, and does not reflect on the operating statement until the inventory is sold, and thus becomes part of the cost of goods sold. Conversely, fixed factory overhead is expensed immediately, and only the variable cost is included in the cost of inventory.

Differences in reported profits will vary as to levels of sales volume and levels of production. For example, when production is higher than sales, higher profits are reported using absorption costing. When sales are higher than production, higher profits are reported using direct costing. Other conditions exist that change reported profits under different costing methods. In cases where both sales and production are equal, both costing methods generally will reflect similar profits. Also, over long periods of time, differences in reported profits will level off, or become less significant.

If we turn our attention to the direct costing statement, you can see that costs are separated between variable and fixed. This brings to light cost behavior by identifying product costs. Through this statement it is possible to simulate conditions by which various segments of different products are changed to reflect the impact of those decisions upon profits. It is through this planning mechanism that the utilization of resources and product mix will be responsible for future profits. At each assumption level the impact on profits will be shown. Those decisions that contribute to profits are accepted, while those resulting in negative profit contribution are rejected. A sampling of some decisions that can take place are presented by the following illustrations.

Referring to the direct costing statement, the following planning decisions are anticipated.

DECISION I

Increase indirect selling expenses by 20%, offset by a 10% increase in sales for product C.

Impact

Higher indirect selling expenses	($315)
Higher product C contribution:	
net sales at $41,000 × 10% increase =	
$4,100 at 50% product contribution	2,050
Increase in operating income	$1,735

DECISION II

Decrease selling price of product A by 10%, offset by a 20% increase in sales for product A.

Impact

Lower product A contribution	
$3,200 lower sales due to 10% reduction in selling price.	($3,200)
Higher product A contribution	
$28,800 ($32,000 − 3,200) of sales at 20% increase in sales (5,760) at a product rate of 36.5%	2,102
Decrease in operating income	($1,098)

DECISION III

Increase sales of product A by 30% and decrease sales of product B by 10%.

Impact

Higher contribution—product A	
$9,600 at 42.8%	$4,109
Lower contribution—product B	
$9,500 at 41.9%	(3,981)
Increase in operating income	$ 128

DECISION IV

Shift in sales of products A and B to product C. Sales efforts will be directed to product C, the more profitable, by decreasing sales of products A and B by 10%, and adding these sales to product C.

Impact

Lower contribution—product A $3,200 at 42.8%	($1,370)
Lower contribution—product B $9,500 at 41.9%	(3,981)
Higher contribution—product C $12,700 at 50.0%	6,350
Increase in operating income	$ 999

The following summarizes the impact on operating income by various decisions. While all these decisions, or the combination thereof, may not occur at the same time, it does illustrate the need for "what if" decisions to determine the impact on earnings.

Decision	Impact on Operating Income	Accepted or Rejected
I	$1,735	Accepted
II	(1,098)	Rejected
III	128	Accepted
IV	999	Accepted
Total	$1,764	

SUMMARY

Note that those decisions resulting in positive operating income would be accepted, such as I, III, and IV; and those contributing operating losses would be rejected, such as decision II. To put these decisions into perspective, it is important to see the impact of these decisions on return-on-investment.

For this illustration we will use the following return-on-investment ratio.

$$\frac{\text{Operating Income}}{\text{Total Assets}}$$

Assuming total assets of $105,000, the original data would show a 27.2% return-on-investment as follows:

$$\frac{\text{Operating Income}}{\text{Total Assets}} = \frac{\$28,560}{\$105,000} = 27.2\%$$

Without any change in total assets, which could change based on the above decisions, the following return-on-investment is calculated reflecting the $1,764 increase to operating income.

$$\frac{\text{Operating Income}}{\text{Total Assets}} = (\$28,560 + 1,764) = \frac{\$30,324}{\$105,000} = 28.9\%$$

You can see how greater productivity is created using the same total assets, and reflecting changes in product mix, price and marketing.

GROSS MARGIN STRATEGY

One way of analyzing earnings is to develop a strategy for increasing gross margins. In reviewing the change of gross margins from one period to another it is important to understand how gross margin is affected. Gross margin represents the difference between net sales and the cost of sales, or the cost to manufacture a product. It plays an important part in the profit strategy by showing how much money is left after manufacturing the product to pay for distributing the product, general and administrative costs, and other costs in operating the business.

The key ratio is the gross margin percent. The following data will be used for illustration and shows a gross margin of 40% for 19X1 and 42% for 19X2. This means that 40 cents and 42 cents, respectively, is available for other costs of operating the business and adequate earnings.

	19X1	19X2	Variance
Units sold	19,500	21,700	2,200
Net sales	$140,000	$168,000	$28,000
Per unit	7.1795	7.7419	.5624
Cost of sales	84,000	97,440	13,440
Per unit	4.3077	4.4903	.1826
Gross margin	$ 56,000	$ 70,560	$14,560
% of net sales	40.0%	42.0%	2.0%

Gross Margin Analysis

From the above, you can see that net sales increased $28,000 due to higher unit sales price (.5624) and higher unit volume (2,200 units). This will be referred to as a sales price and sales volume variance, since both sales volume and price are affected. Cost of sales increased $13,440 due to higher unit costs (.1826) and is referred to as a cost price variance, and higher unit sales of 2,200 units is referred to as a cost volume variance. This analysis will show why gross margin increased $14,560 by attributing this to changes in volume, price and cost.

Sales Price Variance

This variance reflects changes in net sales due to differing unit sales prices between periods. It is accomplished by keeping this period's unit sales constant, and reflecting changes in unit sales prices. The following calculations are made.

This year's units sold at this year's unit
   sales price
        21,700 X $7.7419   = $168,000

This year's units sold at prior year's unit
   sales price
        21,700 X $7.1795   = 155,795
   Favorable sales price variance $ 12,205

Sales Volume Variance

Changes in net sales are reflected due to changes in units sold from one period to another. Prior year's sales price are kept constant, with the variable being units sold. It is calculated as follows:

This year's units sold at prior year's unit
   prices
        21,700 X $7.1795   = $155,795

Prior year's units sold at prior year's
   unit prices
        19,500 X $7.1795   = 140,000
   Favorable sales volume variance $ 15,795

Cost Price Variance

This variance measures the changes that occur in cost of sales between periods, due to changes in the cost of the product. It is calculated as follows.

This period's units sold at this period's
   unit cost of sales
        21,700 X $4.4903   = $97,440

This period's units sold at prior
   period's unit cost of sales
        21,700 X $4.3077   = 93,477
   Unfavorable cost price variance   ($ 3,963)

Note that the units sold for this period do not change, but are reflected in changing cost of sales. Higher unit cost of sales for the current period (.1826) resulted in an unfavorable cost price variance of $3,963.

Cost Volume Variance

This reflects changes in units sold between periods by keeping unit cost of sales constant, and using units sold as a variable. It is calculated as follows.

This year's units sold at prior year's
unit cost of sales
$$21,700 \times \$4.3077 \quad = \quad \$93,477$$

Prior year's units sold at prior
year's unit cost of sales
$$19,500 \times \$4.3077 \quad = \quad \underline{84,000}$$

Unfavorable cost volume variance   ($ 9,477)

SUMMARY

A summary is presented explaining the $14,560 increase in gross margin from 19X1 to 19X2. Each variance will impact upon gross margin with the sum reflecting the total variance.

		Impact on Gross Margin
Net sales variance	$28,000	
Sales price variance		$12,205
Sales volume variance		15,795
Cost of sales variance	(13,440)	
Cost price variance		(3,963)
Cost volume variance		(9,477)
Gross margin variance	$14,560	$14,560

Note that the favorable total variance for gross margin of $14,560 is attributable to the many factors constituting gross margin, namely price, volume, and cost. This analysis will assist in establishing strategy for pricing, marketing, and manufacturing. A balanced combination will result in higher earnings.

STRATEGIES THROUGH
PRODUCT LINE PROFITABILITY

The marketing executive is constantly faced with decisions that reflect the dynamics of the ever-changing business environment. To survive in this business climate, the marketing manager is concerned with such decisions as follows.

What markets and/or products should be eliminated?
What markets and/or products should be expanded?
At what price should the product be sold?
What new markets and/or products should be entered into?
What is the breakeven for territories and products?
How much money should be spent for supporting markets and products?
What information do I need to make these decisions?

We have seen how both revenues and costs are segregated, and how they react directly and indirectly, depending upon the type of cost. In a later chapter on reporting strategies, it will be pointed out how an effective reporting system operates, and the basics of a sound reporting system. Since that chapter deals with the total reporting concept, this chapter will deal with product line strategies, and the information needed to effectively operate as part of a total management information system.

What is needed is a system which takes accounting conventions and principles, and restates the data to provide information by profit segment. For example, data on profit contribution by product is necessary to insure proper price/cost relationship. This is also true by marketing segment of the business. Introducing, deleting, make or buy, products and/or territories are important decisions necessary to focus attention on the desired profit to maintain growth. This system is referred to as profitability accounting. Through this system, various managerial accounting techniques are integrated through detailed reports at various levels of the organization. This data is then used for managerial decisions such as costing of products, pricing, make or buy analysis, profitability analysis, sales analysis, cash flow analysis, return-on-investment, and overall budgeting control.

Previously, we saw how gross margin analysis was broken down into variances of sales price, sales volume, cost price, and cost volume variances. It dealt with analyzing the changes of gross margin from 19X1 to 19X2, and explained the variation as follows:

Gross margin 19X1	$56,000
Net sales variance	
Sales price variance	12,205
Sales volume variance	15,795
Cost of sales variance	
Cost price variance	(3,963)
Cost volume variance	(9,477)
Gross margin 19X2	$70,560

Applying the other operating income and expense variances from 19X1 to 19X2, the following results:

	19X1 vs. 19X2
Net earnings 19X1	$10,600
Increased gross margin	14,560
Increased depreciation	(500)
Increased selling expenses	(1,176)
Increased administrative expenses	(4,368)
Increased general expenses	(956)
Higher other income	(1,120)
Increased interest expenses	(420)
Higher income taxes	(4,060)
Net earnings 19X2	$14,800

In reviewing the above, you can see the impact of each of the elements on net earnings.

It is recognized that the marketing function provides the main ingredient to net earnings, namely, revenues or net sales. Associated with the generation of revenues are related costs which can be specifically identified, and in some cases, not specifically identified. Most expenses are a function of getting a product from manufacturer or distributor to the consumer, and can be managed more effectively through analyzing product contributions.

PRODUCT CONTRIBUTION

Under this concept, the relative product data is presented which represents only identifiable costs to a particular product. Using this format of reporting, management can better understand the effects on the relative profitability of each product, particularly on the effects of increased volume and/or changing prices.

Product Contribution
19X2

		P R O	D U	C T
	Total	A	B	C
Net sales	$168,000	$32,000	$95,000	$41,000
Variable costs	91,000	17,600	53,800	19,600
Variable contribution	77,000	14,400	41,200	21,400
% of net sales	45.8%	45.0%	43.4%	52.2%
Direct fixed costs	3,000	700	1,400	900
Product contribution	$ 74,000	$13,700	$39,800	$20,500
% of net sales	44.0%	42.8%	41.9%	50.0%

The above analysis can also be reviewed from a sales territory, a salesperson, a distributor, or any other viable breakout needed to manage the business.

Return on Controllable Assets

Sales performance is generally measured by unit and/or dollar volume. In most cases, no assignment of investment dollars that are needed to support these sales revenues is used to calculate the financial results. To properly evaluate the return on product contribution, it is important to assign some investment value.

Two major assets that can be considered as investment are inventories and receivables. Inventories are needed to support sales and receivables are a result of sales. Therefore, it is possible to isolate both inventories and receivables by product line, and assign these assets to each product line. Assuming the following assignment of inventories and receivables to each product line, a total investment base can be established.

Controllable Assets
19X2

		P R O	D U	C T
	Total	A	B	C
Receivables	$20,400	$3,800	$11,000	$ 5,600
Inventories	26,400	4,900	14,100	7,400
Total	$46,800	$8,700	$25,100	$13,000

Using the return-on-investment formula of net earnings divided by investment, the following return-on-controllable assets results.

	Total	P R O A	D U C T B	C
Product contribution	$74,000	$13,700	$39,800	$20,500
Controllable assets	$46,800	$ 8,700	$25,100	$13,000
Return on controllable assets	158.1%	157.5%	158.6%	157.7%

Each of the product lines contributes a substantial return on controllable assets. When the other elements comprising net earnings and total assets are applied, the results are as follows:

	Net earnings
Product contribution	$74,000
Indirect fixed expenses	45,440
Operating income	28,560
Income taxes	13,760
Net earnings	$14,800

	Total assets
Cash & marketable securities	$ 20,400
Controllable assets	46,800
Net fixed assets	39,500
Other assets	6,300
Total assets	$113,000

The return on total assets would be 13.1%. It is obvious that by controlling product line return on controllable assets, the total return on total assets will be enhanced. It is therefore established that product line profitability is the key to overall company performance. This same analysis can be developed by territory, major customers, salesperson, and so forth.

Increasing Overall Return

To increase overall return on total assets, several key decisions can be established. However, it must be recognized that these decisions are subject to the constraints of the marketplace, corporate philosophy, and the ability to effectively carry out these programs. Three major decisions can be made as follows.

☐ Increase net sales by price increases on selected products, and changing sales mix to sell more profitable products. Assuming a 10% increase, the product contribution would be increased by 10%, and the effect on return on controllable assets as follows:

Product contribution	$81,400
Controllable assets	$46,800
Return on controllable assets	173.9%
Increase over original data	15.8%

☐ Reduce selling expenses by instituting a more effective cost control program. Assuming a 5% decrease, the following results:

Product contribution	$77,700
Controllable assets	$46,800
Return on controllable assets	166.0%
Increase over original data	7.9%

☐ Reduce receivables and inventories by tighter screening of customers and disposing of obsolete and slow moving products. Assuming a reduction of 5%, the following results:

Product contribution	$74,000
Controllable assets	$44,460
Return on controllable assets	166.4%
Increase over original data	8.3%

Taking all three decisions into consideration, the following results are calculated for both return on controllable assets and return on total assets.

	Original Data	Revised Data
Product contribution	$ 74,000	$ 85,100
Controllable assets	46,800	44,460
Return on controllable assets	158.1%	191.4%
Net earnings		
Product contribution	$ 74,000	$ 85,100
Indirect fixed costs	45,440	45,440
Operating income	28,560	39,660
Income taxes	13,760	19,108
Net earnings	$ 14,800	$ 20,552
Total assets		
Cash & marketable securities	$ 20,400	$ 20,400
Controllable assets	46,800	44,460
Net fixed assets	39,500	39,500
Other assets	6,300	6,300
Total assets	$113,000	$110,660
Return on total assets	13.1%	18.6%

You can see how certain decisions at the product line level can impact on overall return-on-investment. The key to overall success is the product line profitability, and the way management allocates resources to support those product line sales. In the previous example, several decisions were simulated, which resulted in increasing return on assets from 13.1% to 18.6%. The impact that the marketing function can have on total performance is paramount to the effectiveness of operating the business. As indicated, sales volume and/or dollars alone are insufficient to measure performance.

The breakeven concept assumes that a company's level of activity is such that revenues and costs are in balance. Thus, neither a profit nor a loss occurs, but the company is said to be at breakeven. Or to put it another way, the breakeven point is when net sales equal both variable and fixed costs. When expressed either numerically or graphically, the effects can easily be seen of shifts or changes in revenues and costs on the operations of the business. Effective use of this tool can be extremely important as a mechanism in managing the business by providing information for decision-making.

To understand breakeven, it must be recognized that the conventional method of earnings statement presentation cannot be used. For example, the following statement is presented reflecting operating profit.

	19X2
Net sales	$168,000
Operating expenses	
Cost of sales	97,440
Depreciation	3,300
Selling expenses	9,576
Administrative expenses	21,168
General expenses	7,956
Total	139,440
Operating profit	$ 28,560

The above data represents an accurate statement of operating profit for the period 19X2, but must be broken down and expressed in a different form in order to calculate breakeven. The restatement must categorize the elements of costs into variable and fixed.

Variable costs are influenced by volume and move in the same proportion, and therefore, vary directly with volume. Fixed costs are not influenced by volume, and remain generally unchanged regardless of volume levels. The following restatement of the above statement is presented breaking down the cost elements into variable and fixed expenses.

Cost elements	Variable	Fixed	Total
Manufacturing	$86,000	$14,740	$100,740
Selling	5,000	1,576	6,576
Administrative	—	21,168	21,168
General	—	7,956	7,956
Other	—	3,000	3,000
Total	$91,000	$48,440	$139,440
% to net sales	54.2%		

The variable costs can be related as a percent of sales, since they are directly related to volume. For every dollar of sales, $.542 is used to pay for variable costs. On the other hand, fixed costs do not change with volume activity, and remain at the same dollar amount regardless of volume changes. Therefore, fixed costs are stated as total dollars and not as a percent of net sales. However, since 54.2% is needed to pay for variable costs, 45.8% of each sales dollar is available to cover fixed costs. This 45.8% represents the margin, or differential, available to cover fixed expenses and produce a profit. This is referred to as Marginal Income. When this income is stated as a percentage of net sales, it is called the Marginal Income Ratio.

With this general background, it is now possible to use breakeven as a strategy for increasing profit. This concept can take on many variations, but will arrive at the same basic conclusion, that is, at what level of activity does profit begin to materialize.

To understand the basic concept, it is important to review the basic definition. The breakeven point is reached when net sales is equal to the sum of variable and fixed costs. In other words, revenues and expenses are equal. At this point, there is no profit and the formula is shown as follows:

$$\text{Net sales} = \text{Variable costs} + \text{Fixed costs}$$

However, if a level of profit were desired, the formula would be as follows:

$$\text{Net sales} = \text{Variable costs} + \text{Fixed costs} + \text{Profit}$$

Applying this formula with zero profit, and referring to the previous statement of variable and fixed costs, the breakeven in sales is as follows:

$$\text{Breakeven} = \frac{\text{Fixed Costs}}{\text{Marginal Income Ratio}} = \frac{\$48,440}{.458} = \$105,764$$

This means that the sales volume must be $105,764 if no losses, as well as no profits, are to result from operations. This is summarized as follows:

Net sales	$105,764
Less variable costs at 54.2%	57,324
Variable margin	48,440
Less fixed costs	$ 48,440
Total	—

You will note that at the sales level of $105,764, applying variable costs and fixed costs, no profit or losses occur. With this type of analysis, it is possible to reflect the impact on decisions in formulating long-range plans and operational programs. For example, using the original data, but projecting a 5% price decrease and a 10% sales volume increase, the following breakeven results:

Net sales	
Original	$168,000
Projected−1.10 (.95 × $168,000)	175,560
Change	$ 7,560
Variable costs	
Original	$ 91,000
Projected−1.10 (.542 × $168,000)	100,162
Change	$ 9,162
Marginal income rate	
Original	45.8%
Projected	43.0%
Change	2.8%
Fixed costs	
Original	$ 48,440
Projected	$ 48,440
Change	none
Operating profit	
Original	$ 28,560
Projected	26,958
Change	$ 1,602
Breakeven	
Original	$105,764
Projected	112,651
Change	$ 6,887

You can see the decisions to decrease price 5% and increase sales volume 10% result in an additional 6.5% sales volume to break even. This can also be looked at on a product-by-product basis, and the impact these changes would have on profits and breakeven.

Other Methods

Other variations exist in calculating breakeven, but it is important to review some of the commonly used terminology associated with breakeven analysis using the following data:

		Per unit
Unit volume	21,700	
Net sales	$168,000	$7.7419
Variable costs	91,000	4.1935
Variable contribution	77,000	$3.5484
Fixed costs	48,440	
Operating profit	$ 28,560	

Definitions

Contribution margin: Net sales minus variable costs, equals fixed costs plus operating profits

$$\$168,000 - \$91,000 = \$48,440 + \$28,560$$
$$\$77,000 \quad = \quad \$77,000$$

To put it in terms of units, how many units are needed to recover fixed costs, plus the desired operating profits? Using the unit sales and costs resulting in unit contribution margin of $3.5484, the breakeven point in units is as follows:

$$\frac{\text{Fixed expenses} + \text{desired operating profit}}{\text{Unit contribution margin}}$$

or

$$\frac{\$48,440 + \$28,560}{\$3.5484} = 21,700 \text{ units}$$

The proof is as follows:

Net sales (21,700 units at $7.7419)	$168,000
Variable costs (21,700 units at $4.1935)	91,000
Contribution margin	77,000
Less fixed costs	48,440
Desired operating profit	$ 28,560

Note that contribution margin can be expressed in total, as a per unit amount, or as a percentage. In this example, the total contribution margin was $77,000; the per unit amount was $3.5484; and the percentage was 45.8%.

Profit contribution ratio: Contribution margin divided by net sales.

$$\frac{\$77,000}{\$168,000} = 45.8\%$$

Margin of safety: Actual sales minus sales at breakeven, divided by actual sales.

$$\frac{\$168,000 - \$105,764}{\$168,000} = 37.0\%$$

This reflects the amount of sales that can decrease before losses can be expected. If both this percent and the contribution margin percent are low, higher selling prices, and reduced variable expenses are recommended.

The Effect of Changes

The following reflects changes in various components of the breakeven formula.

Volume changes: Assuming that unit volume increases to 25,000 units, what is the effect on operating profit?

$$\$7.7419 \times 25,000 = \$4.1935 \times 25,000 + \$48,440 + X$$
$$\$193,548 = 104,838 + 48,440 + X$$
$$\$193,548 = 153,278X$$
$$X = \$40,270$$

The revised profit is $40,270, or an increase of $11,710 as follows:

Increase in:	
Net sales	$25,548
Variable costs	13,838
Variable contribution	11,710
Less fixed costs	—
Operating profit	$11,710

Cost changes: Assuming fixed costs increase $2,000, with unit sales volume at 21,700 units, and net sales at $168,000, how many units must be sold to avoid a reduction in operating profits ($28,560)?

$$\$7.7419X = \$4.1935X + \$50,440 + \$28,560$$
$$\$3.5484X = \$79,000$$
$$X = 22,264 \text{ units}$$

The additional units to maintain the same amount of operating profit is 564 units. The effect of these additional units on operating profit is as follows:

Increase in:

Net sales	$4,366
Variable costs	2,366
Variable contribution	2,000
Less fixed costs	$2,000
Operating profit	0

Price changes: The effect of price changes on operating profit, or what unit volume changes are needed to maintain the same level of operating profit ($28,560), with a change in unit price from $7.7419 to $9.50?

$$\$9.50X = \$4.1935X + \$48,440 + \$28,560$$
$$\$5.3065X = \$77,000$$
$$X = 14,511 \text{ units}$$

The impact of a price increase of $1.7581 per unit resulted in reducing the number of units to be sold by 33.129%, or 7,189 units as follows:

Reduction in:

Net sales	$30,147
Variable costs	$30,147
Variable contribution	—
Less fixed costs	—
Operating profit	0

Effect of taxes: The calculation used previously reflects the impact before taxes, or operating profit. To reflect the impact of taxes, the following formula would be used:

Net sales = Variable costs + fixed costs + taxes + profit

Assuming a 48% tax rate, and using the original data, the following calculation is presented:

$$\$168,000 = \$91,000 + \$48,440 + (.48 \times \$28,560) + X$$
$$168,000 = 139,440 + 13,709X$$
$$\$168,000 = 153,149X$$
$$X = \$14,851$$

In summary, breakeven reflects relationships that exist between cost, volume, and profit, by measuring the impact of changes. In addition, it assists in developing short and long-term strategies for operating the business. In the short run, corrective actions can take place to turn around an unfavorable condition. In the long run, strategies can be developed to assure financial stability.

STRATEGIES
THROUGH PRICING

Pricing is one of the key decisions that managers must make. Its influence reaches throughout the organization and affects the survival of a company. The ability to balance and maximize both volume and price is needed to provide the financial stability consistent with the stated financial structure as set forth by the company.

The pricing of products must respond to many factors. The marketplace will determine at what price, and at what volume customers will respond. Outside influences such as governmental regulations, legal implications, technological changes, competition, and general economic conditions, will also influence pricing. Producing the product to meet the selling price objective requires determining internal research and development capabilities, as well as investment requirements to manufacture and sell the product at differing volume levels. And most of all, production of the product must provide the profit necessary to sustain growth through decisions involving volume, cost, and price. With the proper combination, profits will materialize.

PRICING STRATEGIES

Many different pricing strategies can be employed to different products, different markets, and may apply to all product lines of a highly diversified company. These strategies can also apply to a particular product in a particular market.

Many companies may use all strategies, since product lines are broad enough to apply to a particular product in a particular market.

In and out—Under this strategy, products are priced at a high value and price reductions instituted when the segment of the market sought after becomes saturated. This can only be effective when there is limited or no competition and substitutes for this product are almost non-existent.

Volume coverage—This approach requires that low margins are accepted, but profits materialize from volume. A product would be directed to reach all segments of the market by setting lower prices, and accomplishing a "low margin, high volume" philosophy.

High prices—Establishing higher than usual prices on selected products may create an image of high quality in the minds of the buying public. This can only be effective in the long run if, in fact, the product is of high quality as compared to competition.

Psychological pricing—The technique of pricing just below the next dollar amount to create the idea in the customers' minds that the product is priced lower than it appears. For example, $12.95, $2.98, and $6.99 appear to be lower than $13.00, $3.00, and $7.00 respectively.

Typical pricing—These are prices which are regarded by the customer as a typical price, such as the price of a package of chewing gum, cigarettes, etc. It is a price that is generally accepted by the customer.

FINANCIAL PRICING

In pricing for profit it is important that considerations be given to decisions which are based on the relationships between volume, cost, price, and profits that result. Several approaches can be used and are discussed below.

Mark-up Approach

Some companies use the mark-up approach which is calculated as follows:

1. The cost of acquiring the product for sale is determined. This may be the cost of purchasing a product in finished, or subassembled form, or the cost of production.
2. The selling and distribution costs are determined, and added to the acquisition or production costs.
3. At this point, it is determined what desired profit is wanted as a dollar amount, or as a percentage of total costs as outlined in #1 and #2 above.

This desired profit is then added to the total costs to determine the selling price.

4. Upon establishing the selling price in step #3, it must then be determined whether this price can sell in that competitive market.

This approach makes no provision for the impact on profit or fixed costs. It applies the same amount of fixed costs regardless of volume, therefore treating fixed costs as a variable expense. In addition, profits are considered variable in relation to volume, and this approach does not allow the opportujity to cost a product based on volume. The more advisable approach is one that deals with price, volume, and cost relationships.

Contribution Approach

This approach brings into focus volume levels and the effect on profits. It utilizes the breakeven concept in that pricing levels are established in keeping with volume levels, fixed costs, and profits desired. Previous chapters dealt with this concept. However, we can develop an example which will deal with these aforementioned concepts. Assuming that the demand for this product is established at differing price levels, the following is presented:

Product Demand

Price Levels	Estimated Sales Units	Estimated Revenues
$6.25	28,800	$180,000
6.75	27,400	184,950
7.25	24,900	180,525
7.75	21,700	168,175
8.25	18,000	148,500
8.75	15,300	133,875
$9.25	10,000	$ 92,500

Assuming the above product demand at various price levels, the following represents the appropriate cost data for each level of estimated sales units.

Product Supply

Estimated Sales Units	Variable Cost Per Unit—$4.1935	Fixed Costs	Total Costs
28,800	$120,773	$48,440	$169,213
27,400	114,902	48,440	163,342
24,900	104,418	48,440	152,858
21,700	90,999	48,440	139,439
18,000	75,483	48,440	123,923
15,300	64,161	48,440	112,601
10,000	$ 41,935	$48,440	$ 90,375

Combining both product demand (revenues) and product supply (costs), the contribution by various levels of volume and price are presented:

Product Profitability

Estimated Sales Units	Price Levels	Estimated Revenues	Total Costs	Product Contribution	Contribution Percent
28,800	$6.25	$180,000	$169,213	$10,787	6.0%
27,400	6.75	184,950	163,342	21,608	11.7
24,900	7.25	180,525	152,858	27,667	15.3
21,700	7.75	168,175	139,439	28,736	17.1
18,000	8.25	148,500	123,923	24,577	16.6
15,300	8.75	133,875	112,601	21,274	15.9
10,000	$9.25	$ 92,500	$ 90,375	$ 2,125	2.3%

The optimum volume and price is 21,700 units at $7.75. At this level, the most contribution is generated. This is also true when computing product contribution as a percent of estimated revenues (17.1%). When more than one product is involved, the same concept can be used by taking the optimum volume and price from each product. This is summarized as follows:

Product	Variable Unit Costs (a)	Optimum Price (b)	Volume at Optimum Price (c)	Product Contribution (d) = c(b − a)	Contribution % of Total
H	$4.1935	$7.75	21,700	$77,176	39.3%
I	6.0213	6.80	23,000	17,910	9.1
J	3.5098	4.75	25,000	31,005	15.7
K	2.7461	3.50	27,000	20,355	10.3
L	$8.4983	$11.30	18,000	50,431	25.6
				$196,877	100.0%
			Other fixed costs	150,000	
			Operating profit	$ 46,877	

The above reflects product costs and the impact on operating profit. Two products, product H and product L, account for 64.9% of the total product contribution. Assuming that concentration is given to these products due to the impact upon the total company, consideration must be given to what production trade-offs exist between these products given certain production constraints.

Before a company can maximize its products to produce the highest contribution, production limitations must be reviewed. In the following example, both product H and product L are produced simultaneously, and total production facilities are limited to 39,700 units. Using various combinations of production which would add up to 39,700 units, the following is presented:

Product H

Units Produced	Contribution Per Unit*	Profit Contribution
15,300	$4.5565	$69,714
18,000	4.0565	73,017
21,700	3.5565	77,176
24,900	3.0565	76,107
27,400	$2.5565	$70,048

Product L

Units Produced	Contribution Per Unit*	Profit Contribution
24,400	$1.8017	$43,961
21,700	2.3017	49,947
18,000	2.8017	50,431
14,800	3.3017	48,865
12,300	$3.8017	$46,761

*Contribution per unit differences result from
lower prices at higher volumes.

Combining both product lines at different production levels, but maintaining a total production level of 39,700 units, the following product contribution results:

Units Produced		Profit Contribution		Total Profit Contribution
Product H	Product L	Product H	Product L	
15,300	24,400	$69,714	$43,961	$113,675
18,000	21,700	73,017	49,947	122,964
21,700	18,000	77,176	50,431	127,607
24,900	14,800	76,107	48,865	124,972
27,400	12,300	$70,048	$46,761	$116,809

The most profitable combination is the optimum level previously discussed, namely, 21,700 units of product H, and 18,000 units of product L. The least profitable is 15,300 units of product H and 24,400 units of product L. Similar analysis can be presented to reflect any combination of product lines, and should be part of the production and pricing decisions.

In summary, pricing should be a key element in the decisions of any company. Pricing will provide the basis for a profitable and well managed company, and provide the financial stability necessary to survive in a highly competitive environment.

STRATEGIES
THROUGH BUDGETING

A budget is a management tool of estimates encompassing all phases of a company's operation over a specified period of time. It generally follows organizational lines of authority, and is structured in accordance with the reporting of accounting data. It is a control and forecasting device which serves as a vehicle for coordinating the efforts of a company. It is as if a company were preparing financial statements in the future, and all the anticipated actions were carried out in a predetermined manner. Therefore, the term budgeting refers to all the processes of preparing a budget, the control thereof, the reporting of actual data versus budget, and all the policies and procedures needed to accomplish the stated objectives.

Definitions

Many terms and expressions are used that relate to the budgeting process. Some of these are used interchangeably. The following terms are most commonly used in business.

Budget—as explained above, a budget is a formal expression of the plans and objectives of management covering all phases of operations for a specific period of time.

Operating budget—an estimate of activity, both revenues and expenses, and other elements of the company, usually for the current period of operations.

Budgeting—refers to the entire process of budget preparation which includes the planning, review, monitoring, and reporting process.

Forecast—a projection of activity for a specified period of time.

ADVANTAGES

The many advantages of budgeting are listed below. They represent the generally accepted advantages found in most organizations using budgeting as a management process. Keep in mind that effective budgeting generally will result in improved profits.

Measures performance along organizational lines—To properly evaluate an organization, it is important that the organization be structured so that functions are held accountable, and therefore capable of being measured. A budgeting process will follow organizational lines, and in fact, may point out deficiencies in organizational structure.

Participation—Since budgeting requires the support of top management, as well as all levels of the organization, the accomplishment of stated objectives will be enhanced. This is true since participation is required at all levels, and therefore builds a team process of management.

Enhances the thinking process—Since objectives must be established by all managers, all facets of the business which the manager is accountable and responsible for, must be considered. The manager develops the logical sequences of events in accomplishing those stated objectives. The budget also brings together thinking that is in coordination with the rest of the organization, so that all of the pieces needed to accomplish those objectives are in harmony.

Goals criteria—Establishes the guidelines for what is acceptable as an objective, and establishes the measurement tools for evaluating those goals.

Resource allocation—Provides the mechanism to properly allocate manpower, facilities, and capital resources to their most economical use.

Re-evaluations—Forces management to constantly re-evaluate budgeted objectives, and adjust to changing conditions.

Like most functions of an organization, there exist limitations which must be recognized. Keep in mind that many of these limitations are related to lack of top management support. Greater management support will overcome many of these limitations, or at the very best, create a workable environment in which budgeting can operate effectively. The following represents some of these recognized limitations.

Measures estimates in quantitative results—Most budgets are measured in dollar or quantitative amounts, and therefore many functions of an organization, such as ability to manage, meeting time commitments, staff development, etc., may go unrecognized.

Accuracy of data—Since budgets are based on estimates, the success or failure of a budget depends upon the accuracy of the estimates. Estimates with sound judgment and business knowledge will generally produce sound management budgets.

Budgeting will not replace sound management—Too often, management inadvertently assumes that what is presented in the budget will materialize. Budgeting represents the guidelines anticipated by each part of the organization, but will not be a substitute for sound management practices. Management's action will determine the effectiveness of the budget.

Limited to the extent of top management support—The budget will only be good as the support management is willing to give in carrying out the planned programs. Without support from all of top management, the organization will not respond, and objectives will not be accomplished.

Budget must be dynamic—It is commonly recognized that business is constantly changing. Economic conditions change, the marketplace changes, and methods of doing business change. To meet these changing conditions, a budgeting program must be flexible to meet these changes in which techniques, methods, and procedures are instituted, worked into the system, reviewed and either continued as part of the budgeting system, or replaced with another more effective way.

Can stifle initiative—The term budgeting sometimes has an unfavorable connotation. It is sometimes thought of as an infringement in managing the business, since it forces commitment and performance standards based on those commitments. If the budgeting system is not considered a tool to help managers perform more effectively, initiative can be stifled. Communication and training are important in helping managers to understand and accomplish the established goals.

METHODS OF ESTABLISHING BUDGETS

Most organizations employ one or both methods of constructing a budget. The method used will depend upon the approach management needs to effectively operate the business. Both approaches, top-down and bottom-up, are sound approaches, but have different advantages and disadvantages.

Top-down approach—Under this method, corporate goals and budgets are generated by a central corporate staff. The results are then allocated back to the divisions for implementing objectives relating to revenues and profits. This method allows for corporate goals to be reflected in the budgets, and can simplify the budgeting effort. However, due to a limited knowledge of the central staff, improper commitments may result at the divisional level.

Bottom-up approach—As the name implies, this approach begins at the operating level, and is built up at each level of the organization. This allows all levels of management to participate and commit objectives at the operating level. However, this requires a great deal of time, since each manager must provide details of each activity of that business. At that level, corporate objectives may not be reflected.

Combination of both methods—A more effective approach would be to combine both approaches by having the operating units use a bottom-up approach, and by obtaining feedback and approval from corporate managers using the top-down approach. Another approach would be to have certain objectives at the corporate level and submitted to the operating managers (top-down), and budgets prepared based on certain objectives, and submitted to corporate managers (bottom-up). Approval or disapproval would then be filtered back to operating managers (top-down), and the process continues for any further actions.

TYPES OF BUDGETS

Since budgeting represents an "operating master plan" by providing the plans and objectives of all parts of the organization, many different types of budgets are needed. They represent different functional areas, as well as varying accountability and responsibility centers. The following represents some of the major types of budgets needed to develop an organization's "master plan."

Sales budget

Represents the revenues anticipated by the company. It may be broken down by products (units and prices), by segments of the market, by territory, and by salesmen. Along with this data, marketing strategies must be provided to support how the revenues will be generated. Since revenues provide the basis for the company to operate, it is important that other considerations be given in support of how the revenues will be obtained. Such areas include the economic environment and general business conditions, anticipated share of market, industry environment, competitive conditions, and impact of governmental regulations.

Manufacturing budget

This budget must be tied in very closely with the sales budget. Inventory must be available to provide for the anticipated units to be sold. This budget will spell out all the costs of manufacturing a product, namely, material, labor, and overhead.

Human resource budget

This budget provides the human resource requirements by detailing headcount, salaries and wages, and employees benefits, for all functions of the organization. It also provides monies allocated for training and development, and future manpower requirements.

Administrative budget

Reflects all expenses of administrative departments such as salaries and wages, employee benefits, travel and entertainment, training and development, memberships, subscriptions, etc. This budget will be prepared by the department which will generate the expense. In addition, strategies must be presented in keeping with the overall budget as to how each administrative department will service the plans of other operating departments, for example manpower additions and reorganization.

Cash budget

This budget provides one of the most important inputs for operating the business. The inputs are derived from all areas of the company, and indicate whether outside financing is necessary. The cash budget indicates whether money is available internally for meeting anticipated capital expenditures as outlined in the capital program. It will reflect operating expenditures, including financing repayments and dividend payments, and revenues to be received from various sources to supply the funds for meeting cash requirements of the company. Two different methods can be used in developing cash budgets, namely, the cash receipts and disbursements method and the adjusted income method.

Cash receipts and disbursements method

This method presents a detailed method of effectively controlling cash by projecting classifications of both cash receipts and cash disbursements. It also is a valuable tool for the timing of estimated cash receipts and disbursements. The following is a simplified example of this type of budget.

Estimated cash receipts—Total receipts estimated from sales, both cash and on account, and other income, such as interest. This amount is then deducted from estimated cash disbursements.

Estimated cash disbursements—Total cash disbursements made from operations, such as payroll and related expenses, payables, general and administrative expenses, selling and advertising expenses, capital expenditure payments, bank loan repayments, and so forth.

The balance, or estimated excess of cash receipts over cash disbursements, or cash disbursements over cash receipts, is added to or subtracted from the beginning cash balance of the period. At this point, a new cash balance is arrived at the period end.

Adjusted income method. This method adjusts net earnings to a cash basis by adding or subtracting all transactions that affect or do not affect cash. For example, depreciation is a non-cash item, and is added back to net earnings in converting back to a cash basis. Addition to net earnings represent non-cash items, decreases in asset balances, and increases in liability balances. Deductions to net earnings represent increases in asset balances and decreases in liability balances. The difference is either added to or subtracted from the beginning cash balance of the period, resulting in a new ending cash balance for the end of the period.

Capital expenditures budget

The capital expenditures budget represents the process by which proposed capital investments are formally presented, and involves large sums of money, long periods of time, and future profits. All costs for each project are presented, including working capital requirements and revenues anticipated. The capital expenditures budget will also include alternatives, and the implication thereof, and expected returns from future earnings generated from the project. Projects are generally classified in one of the following categories:

Growth and expansion—includes such projects as new facilities and new products, expansion of existing facilities and products, entry into new markets and new products, product improvements, product capacity, and technological changes. These types of projects produce earnings and contain substantial risks.

Replacements—projects needed to continue or maintain the business. This includes not only replacements, but repairs and maintenance. Evaluation is dependent upon potential loss of earnings, and is sometimes difficult to measure.

Cost reduction—as the name implies, cost savings can be justified and measured, and present a potential return to the company in the form of higher earnings.

Other—includes projects where quantitative data is difficult to measure, such as for employee morale and safety. While no immediate tangible benefits can be highlighted, it is recognized that these investments are necessary and provide employee satisfaction, and ultimately, higher productivity and earnings. A balance of these projects is necessary in the total capital expenditures budget, since monies must be carefully allocated to projects offering tangible returns that can be identified.

The above classifications generally will fit most major categories. Additional classifications and terminology may be also used.

STRATEGIES THROUGH
CAPITAL SPENDING

One of the key elements of a company's growth is investments in assets. When you look at most companies, all products and services have a life cycle. That is not to say that the life cycle is short. It means that technological, environmental, sociological, and economic changes may cause a product's life cycle to end at any point in the cycle. Therefore, it is important to reinvest monies earned back into the business in the form of assets both to replenish goods and services, and to provide new goods and services that have reached the end of their life. In some cases, it is necessary to borrow funds to finance opportunities that are projected to generate a return over and above the stated objectives.

Investments in assets take many different forms. They may be of a functional nature, such as to support the sales effort, production requirements, distribution, or administrative needs. There are no guidelines for a company's investments in functional areas as long as funds can be made available, and justification can be supported. The types of investments that can be in support of these functional areas are as follows:

Physical assets—As the name implies, these are tangible assets needed to support the production of goods and services. They include acquiring land, as well as land improvements, machinery and equipment, office equipment, and transportation equipment.

Working capital—Most capital expenditures require additional working capital. (Working capital is defined as current assets less current liabilities.) Such additions to working capital would include cash requirements, build-ups of receivables and inventories in support of increased sales, and increased payables to pay for these build-ups in assets.

Other investments—Other investments may be necessary to support both physical assets and working capital. They include investments in research and development, such as for scientific, marketing, production, financial and economic research, and certain expenses which would be part of the capital costs of any investment deemed to be capitalized by accounting principles.

You can see that investments take on many different roles. One tends to think of investments in physical assets only, when in fact, supporting investments play a major role in the capital investment process. In computing capital needs, these elements must be considered as part of the total capital investment package.

INVESTMENT VARIABLES

Before any investment is considered, many factors must be considered. They are factors that must rank the investment as to its importance, so that priorities can be established as to which factors play a major role. The investment decision will involve many variables as discussed below. The order is not indicative of importance, but merely a listing of factors to be considered in a "go" or "no go" decision.

Profitability—many decisions are based on economic desirability as set forth in operating objectives. These objectives were previously discussed, and provide the basis for establishing cut-off criteria.

Impact on company—capital investments will impact the company's structure in many ways, depending upon how important the investment is to the total company. A major investment may require financial structuring. Determination must be made as to the effect on the short and long-term financial position. Will the "eggs in one basket" situation be present? How will our competitors react to any competitive edge we may enjoy through this investment?

Positioning—does the investment position itself in the environment for which it is intended? Consideration must also be given to the timing of the investment. Is this the right time to embark upon a new product, or will technology shorten the product's life? Will the new machinery meet with technological change? These are a few of the considerations necessary to evaluate the positioning aspect.

Political, social, and economic environment—consideration must be given to factors outside the company's environment. Investments made internally are affected by outside factors. For example, such key issues as economic policies may determine the aggressiveness to meet or expand the business. Money costs, inflation, unemployment and general economic conditions, will be major factors in certain investment decisions. Consideration must also be given to the political climate when dealing with local areas as to major investments, particularly in plant expansions or plant relocations.

Legal considerations—it is advisable that investments be reviewed by the legal department. Implications may exist that would put a company in jeopardy on certain investments. Size and the nature of the investment will dictate the extent to which the legal department will be involved.

Project content—the content of the project must contain the best available data, enabling the reviewer to make the proper decison. The decision reached will be dependent upon the reliability of the data, and in some cases, prior experience relating to this particular project. The project should contain alternatives, and the consequences of risk should be kept in mind. What would be the consequences of failure, or the impact of success?

Image and character—certain projects must be reviewed in relation to the image and character of the company. These images are viewed by the customer, industry, and the investor, and assist in providing the direction set forth in the company's objectives. Since most companies have established an image by which they operate, plans are established along these lines, therefore investments will be in accordance with the long-range character and plans of the company.

Qualitative factors—other factors such as environmental responsibility, the safety of employees, goals of management, and employee morale, must also be considered. These factors are of a qualitative nature, since numerical justification would be difficult to obtain. However, they cannot be ignored and may in fact be a determining factor.

The above variables will be part of the decision process to accept or reject an investment opportunity. As indicated, the relative importance of these variables will depend upon the investment being considered.

THE CAPITAL INVESTMENT PROCESS

The process of investing in capital expenditures usually follows a logical sequence. This sequence starts with an idea, and ends with a decision, and then a review of the results expected against what has materialized. Its simplicity is logical. If you have a problem, find out what it is, what actions are necessary to remedy the problem, and act upon it. With this simple analogy, let's examine the steps in sequence. It is important to note that other interim steps may be necessary, but will still follow this process.

1. *Identify problem or opportunity search*—Within the organization, problems or opportunities may arise. At this point, the problem is defined and presented, or the opportunity is explored and presented. In either case, the process is started.

2. *Alternatives*—Based on the problem or opportunities presented, alternatives are explored and presented with the prior data. The consequences of each alternative are measured and weighted against each other. A decision is reached as to the recommended alternative, and stated in the presentation.

3. *Applicability to future plans*—The data presented must be evaluated in keeping with the long-term plans and objectives of the company. This is considered so as to assure continuing future development in terms of markets, product lines, philosophy, and projected size of the company. The long-range plans, including capital investment requirements, will highlight these factors.

4. *Capital expenditure budget*—Based on the investment proposals, a capital expenditures budget is prepared which would include the nature of the investment, such as type, urgency, and impact, amount of funds required for the investment, working capital and expenses, economic justification, such as payback, discounted cash flow, etc., estimated starting date, time schedule of estimated cash payments, and authorizations necessary. This would be supported by documentation for each proposal as outlined in the company's policy and procedure.

5. *Approval process*—Proposals would be accepted or rejected based on the economics and strategy objectives set forth by the company. Those projects that did not meet this criteria would be rejected, and those that did, would be accepted. Availability of funds and ultimate risk would also be major factors.

6. *Controls*—On those approved projects, controls must be established to assure that outlays of cash are in keeping with those expenditures authorized. Projects not started in the budget year approved must be resubmitted as a new proposal, and compete with other investment proposals also submitted for that budget year. Approval of projects is not a license to commit funds beyond the year in which it is intended. Therefore, controls must be established for this reason, as well as cash control.

7. *Post-completion*—Much has been spoken about post-completion audits. The process of evaluating actual performance of a project as compared to its estimate is a long discussed problem. Monitoring the project in the stages of completion is well advised. Review after completion is also well advised. However, reviewing the project over a long period of time against

what was estimated may defeat the purpose. Accountability generally will have changed, and the originators and approvers may have other functions. At that point, should blame for not meeting estimates be directed to individuals possibly not having that responsibility? More importantly, it is recognized that when projects are completed, they become part of the normal process of evaluating operations. Caution should be given to at what stage, how long, and with what intensity, projects will be post audited.

8. *Disposals*—At all times, assets must be considered as candidates for disposals. Whether they are idle, non-productive, obsolete, or unprofitable, they need to be part of a program for disposal. In many cases this arises out of acquiring new investments, and the asset becomes available for disposal. A continuing program is suggested which would also include disposal of total operations which do not meet overall objectives, or do not fit the strategies of the company.

9. *Policy and procedure review*—Constant updates must be carried on to assure that both policies of the company, as well as procedures, are in keeping with what is planned. To change cut-off profitability requirements without changing the policies, is counterproductive. Procedures should change to meet new reporting requirements, including forms and routings of approval. In summary, the process must meet the requirements and structure of the organization. Most companies develop a different style that works most effectively in the organization.

FIXED ASSET OBJECTIVES

The acquisiton of fixed assets requires sound planning and control techniques. As indicated previously, the importance of acquiring fixed assets is paramount to the future survival of the company. Therefore, accurate determination must be made as to the economic values projected, or in some cases, continuation of the business. The following represents the planning and control objectives in the acquisition of fixed assets, and is reflected in the capital budget program of the company.

Economic worth—reviewing the estimated financial returns on projects, and choosing those projects which offer the greatest returns. This is in keeping with return-on-investment objectives as set forth by corporate policy. However, there may be circumstances where economic worth may not be a factor, such as the replacement of an asset. In this case, decisions must be reached as to what are the consequences of not replacing, and what type of replacement is necessary in light of the marketplace, technology, and production costs.

Financial support—the capital program will match requested capital expenditures and available funds necessary to support these expenditures. The process of elimination will usually be determined by the cut-off rate of return and financial capabilities. However, where opportunity presents itself, additonal financial risk may be necessary to take advantage of additional opportunities, over and above the financial capabilities. This determination must be reviewed very cautiously.

Compatibility—with short and long-range plans of the company. Acquisition of fixed assets must tie-in with plans as spelled out in corporate objectives. Recommending buying a plant non-related to the objectives of the company would not be accepted. However, if the plant can produce a return beyond what is normally expected, corporate objectives may be changed to accommodate such an investment. While fixed assets should relate to corporate objectives, do not rule out attractive investments. Many companies entered new fields of business through this very process.

Coordination—relating the timeliness of the acquisition, as well as other functional areas being affected—for example, buying a new piece of equipment to double production where neither the sales force is adequate, nor the marketplace big enough to handle the added production—would not be a wise decision. All areas of the company being affected must be coordinated before commitments are made.

Justification—needed to determine whether new fixed assets can be financially justified, as well as the needs for the asset being acquired. Financial justification techniques will be discussed later.

Control—should be exercised to assure that monies are expended in accordance with authorizations established. In addition, it is important to establish the necessary approval levels, usually coordinated in conjunction with the type and amount of the project. Accountability for performance must also be established, so that monitoring and evaluation will take place during, and upon completion of the fixed asset acquired. Results need to be compared with the projections that were submitted and approved.

SUMMARY

In summary, establishing over-all objectives for planning and control of acquiring fixed assets will lead to more effective and profitable business decisions. Companies that fail are often lacking in this area of operating a business. With this brief background on the capital spending process, the next chapter will deal with the capital expenditure evaluation process. Techniques of evaluation will be explored to provide the reader with a working knowledge of this evaluation process.

CAPITAL EXPENDITURE
EVALUATION STRATEGIES

The capital evaluation process provides the mechanism to choose those capital investments that are projected to generate the greatest return to the company. The process uses techniques generally accepted in business, and provides the company with numerical values in terms of time to recover the initial investment, and a return-on-investment rate. This rate is compared to the company's over-all objective or cut-off rate, and approval or disapproval follows accordingly. While this is a brief summary, most capital expenditures involve the preparing of the capital request, the evaluation and approval phase, and the follow-up phase. It is recognized that many capital evaluation techniques can be used. We will deal with those most generally accepted.

PREREQUISITES
OF EVALUATION TECHNIQUES

To properly evaluate capital investment proposals, many factors must be present. Most companies will use methods that offer the facts for decision-making that meet the style of management currently present within the organization.

The style will dictate the policies and procedures for developing capital investment proposals in relation to the techniques used, method of presentation, and approval process. To say that one method or evaluation technique is better than others is short-sighted. However, several techniques have been tested, and are regarded as the most generally accepted. In addition, it is also generally accepted that those methods used will adhere to the following prerequisites.

Easy to understand and calculate—Whatever method used, it must be easily understood, and easy to calculate by all individuals within the organization who would have the need to be involved, either in the preparation, or approval process. This means that the techniques used must be adaptable to all parts of the organization, and capable of being used for all projects within the organization. A method that is easy to calculate, easy to understand, and adaptable to all project situations, will generally be universally accepted throughout the organization.

Elements of risk—All methods should be capable of measuring risk. This can be accomplished by building in the judgment of risk by management in the preparation of the capital investment proposal. Cut-off or hurdle rates can be adjusted to reflect the riskiness of the project, i.e. higher the risk, higher the hurdle rate. Another technique is to adjust cash flows using probability estimates, such as, what are the probability estimates of achieving projected cash flows? In this case, cash flows are adjusted by high, low, and most probable estimates, and a single cash flow calculation is arrived at.

Recovery calculation—As part of the evaluation process, a calculation of how long it will take to recover the initial investment should be made. This is commonly referred to as payback. As explained later, payback does not compute return-on-investment, but merely is an indicator of cash recoverability. Therefore, this calculation is used in conjunction with other methods of calculation, such as discounted cash flow.

Time value of money—Calculation should include the impact of the time value of money. This is generally accomplished through using discounted cash flow techniques. Using this method will also require that cash flows be generated for the life of the project. This will require calculating all cash flows for the entire estimated life of the project which may be based on obsolescence, technology, or economic values.

The above presents some of the most commonly accepted prerequisites. When all are considered and utilized, they provide the basis for a sound and acceptable way of measuring capital investment proposals.

Cash flow represents the key ingredient in the calculating of capital investment proposals. From cash flows, such techniques as payback and discounted
cash flow are calculated. To properly evaluate the economics of capital projects,
various elements must be calculated to arrive at net cash flows. The concept of
cash flow used for this purpose will be calculated as follows:

net earnings (as reported in the earnings statement)

plus

depreciation (periodic amount dependent upon method)

Note that depreciation is added back to net earnings, even though it does not
represent a source of cash, but provides cash by reducing income taxes. To show
the impact of this statement, the following example is presented of two
situations—one situation having depreciation, and the other without a charge to
earnings for depreciation.

	Without Depreciation	With Depreciation
Net sales	$168,000	$168,000
Operating expenses	136,140	136,140
Depreciation		3,300
Operating profit	31,860	28,560
Other income	2,520	2,520
Interest expense	2,520	2,520
Income before provision for income taxes	31,860	28,560
Provision for income taxes	15,350	13,760
Net earnings	$ 16,510	$14,800
Differential	└── $1,710 ──┘	

Note that the additional cash flow of $1,710 is provided through the reduction
of income taxes.

In addition, net cash flows include investment expenditures for fixed
assets, as well as for working capital. To partially offset the investment expenditures, salvage values at the end of the life of the asset must be considered. This
would have the effect of generating more cash flows.

Taking all these factors into consideration, net cash flows would include
the following, and impact on either the balance sheet or the earnings statement.

Effect on

Earnings statement and
    Balance sheet   number of periods (based on life of the
                                  project)

Balance sheet	investment expenditures (includes working capital)
Balance sheet	salvage values
Earnings statement	revenues
Earnings statement	reduction of expenses
Earnings statement	operating expenses
Earnings statement	depreciation
Earnings statement	other income and expense
Earnings statement	taxes
Earnings statement	net earnings

The above represents net cash flows and includes all the elements needed to financially evaluate a capital investent proposal. It is these net cash flows that money is provided for, or anticipated to be received. It is usually recognized that money is needed initially to finance the investment being acquired. Future time periods will provide the funds to recover this investment and to operate the business. Where funds are needed, they may be obtained through many sources—internal operations, borrow from a lending institution (i.e. bank, insurance, etc.), sell marketable securities, or defer making short-term payments. Any combination of these cash generators would be accepted, but must be in keeping with corporate policy, philosophy, and the ability to attract capital in those mentioned money markets.

PAYBACK METHOD

The payback method is most commonly used, and is referred to as the payback period method, cash recovery period method, payout, payoff, and the payback method. This method is easy to calculate and understand, measures recoverability, is an excellent indicator of cash risk, and gives greater weight to cash flows projected in the earlier periods. However, it must be noted that payback is not a true rate of return. It measures the time necessary to recover the initial investment from net cash flows, and gives no weight to net cash flows beyond the payback period.

The following data will be used to illustrate the payback method, and other succeeding methods discussed in this chapter.

Initial investment	$25,000
Life of project	5 years
Straight-line depreciation	
No salvage value	

Yearly cash flows

Year 1	$10,000
Year 2	9,000
Year 3	8,000
Year 4	7,000
Year 5	6,000

The payback calculation is as follows:

$$\frac{\text{Initial investment}}{\text{Yearly cash flows}} = \text{number of years necessary to equal the initial investment}$$

or

$$\frac{\$25,000}{\$10,000 + \$9,000 + (\$6,000 \div \$8,000)} = 2.75 \text{ years}$$

You can see that two full years of cash flows will recover $19,000 ($10,000 + $9,000) of the initial investment, and $6,000 remains to be recovered. Therefore, an additional $6,000 is needed from the cash flow of year 3 of $8,000. Dividing $6,000 by $8,000 will give a partial year of .75 years. The payback period is then calculated at 2.75 years.

Applying discounted cash flow techniques, which will be discussed later, the following calculation can be made.

		Present Value	Present Values	
Year	Cash Flows	Factors at 15%	Yearly	Cumulative
0	($25,000)	1.000	($25,000)	($25,000)
1	10,000	.870	8,700	(16,300)
2	9,000	.756	6,804	(9,496)
3	8,000	.658	5,264	(4,232)
4	7,000	.572	4,004	(228)
5	6,000	.497	2,982	$ 2,754
	$15,000		$ 2,754	

The discounted payback period is 4.076 years, calculated as follows:

		Amount of net
	Years	cash flows
Number of full years	4.000	$24,772
Remaining to recover		228
Partial year ($228 ÷ $2,982)	.076	
Total payback period	4.076	$25,000

This compares to 2.75 years previously calculated. The difference of 1.326 years represents the value placed upon the time value of money, which states that money is worth more today than in the future.

This method is the easiest to calculate of the methods in computing the return-on-investment of a capital investment. The other method, discounted cash flow, will be discussed later. The accounting method of evaluation compares accounting data to forecasted data based on generally accepted accounting principles. Unlike the discounted cash flow method, no effort is made to measure both accounting and forecasted data using discounting techniques. This is true, since no discounting is taken into consideration. Several terms have been used in describing the accounting method, such as the book value rate of return, accounting rate of return, approximate rate of return, and the unadjusted rate of return. They all relate to data used in accordance with accounting principles and practices.

Attention should be paid to the fact that not all individuals are familiar with accounting data. In addition, this method gives equal weight to all cash flows for all years, assumes the project will last its entire life, and ignores any time value of money. Using the previous data, the cash flows must be adjusted to reflect net earnings only for each period, as well as the total. This will result in measuring return-on-investment for capital projects as follows:

$$\frac{\text{Total net earnings}}{\text{Initial investment}}$$

There are variations that can exist with the above, such as using annual earnings, average investment, average book values, etc. For illustration purposes, we will assume that total net earnings for the life of the project and initial investment will be used. If other variations are selected, then either the numerator, denominator, or both must be changed. The following assumes straight-line depreciation over a five year life.

Year	Cash Flows	Depreciation	Net Earnings
1	$10,000	$ 5,000	$ 5,000
2	9,000	5,000	4,000
3	8,000	5,000	3,000
4	7,000	5,000	2,000
5	6,000	5,000	1,000
	$40,000	$25,000	$15,000

Note that one component of cash flow was eliminated, namely, depreciation. This resulted in net earnings per period. Since depreciation is part of cash flow, the results logically represent only net earnings. Using the net earnings data above, the return-on-investment for this capital proposal is 60% as follows:

$$\frac{\$15,000}{\$25,000} = 60\%$$

To properly use this method, all capital projects must be evaluated the same way. In other words, be consistent in evaluation techniques.

DISCOUNTED CASH FLOW

The theory of discounted cash flow (DCF) says that a dollar today is worth more than a dollar in the future. This method uses the interest rate, and indicates what percentage return an investor may expect on those funds to be recovered or generated each year, over the life of the project. This is the risk that an investor assumes when investing in a company, by providing funds for management to invest. Assuming that most companies generally need some outside financing, funds may be generated from outside sources at a specific rate, or from future cash flows from past, present, and future projects. The interest rate is easily identified from outside sources, but is assumed to be the rate assigned under DCF for internal funds generated from capital projects. Therefore, it assumes that those cash flows can be reinvested at the discount rate.

When using DCF, there are many terms which also refer to the discounting concept. These terms all consider the time value of money, require forecasted cash flows for all periods within the project's life, and provide a basic common ground for varying types of projects. The terms sometimes used are net present value, time adjusted rate of return, investor's method, interest rate of return, present worth, profitability index, margin efficiency of capital, the scientific method, and discounted cash flow. It must be recognized that in computing DCF, the uncertainty of forecasted cash flows exists, and when these cash flows are discounted, they will not relate to accounting records for comparative purposes.

Compounding

To understand the concept of discounting, it is important to understand compounding. Compounding is shifting the value of money from the present into the future. To illustrate, let's assume you deposit $1.00 in a savings account at 8% annual interest. How much will you have after five years?

Year	Principal	Interest-8%	Total
0	$1.00	—	$1.00
1	1.00	$ .08	1.08
2	1.08	.09	1.17
3	1.17	.09	1.26
4	1.26	.10	1.36
5	$1.36	$ .11	$1.47

The answer is $1.47. Without calculating each year's total, reference could be made to a compound interest table as follows:

Compound Interest
Table at 8%

Year	Compound Factor
0	1.000
1	1.080
2	1.166
3	1.260
4	1.360
5	1.469

The same answer can be arrived at by applying the compound interest factor of 1.469 to the principal of $1.00. See appendix for compound interest tables.

Discounting

The reverse of compounding is discounting. Under the discounting concept, the value of money to be received in the future is shifted back to the present. Taking the same $1.00 at 8%, and applying the discounting concept, the question is now reversed. If I need $1.00 in 5 years, how much must I deposit today, earning 8% annual interest? The following illustration provides the answer.

Year	Principal	Interest-8%	Total
0	$1.47	1.000	$1.47
1	1.47	.926	1.36
2	1.47	.857	1.26
3	1.47	.794	1.17
4	1.47	.735	1.08
5	$1.47	.681	$1.00

The answer is also $1.47. Reference could also be made to the discount, or present value table to determine the factor to be used in arriving at $1.47. An example of the 8% present value table is presented.

Present Value
Table at 8%

Year	Present Value Factor
0	1.000
1	.926
2	.857
3	.794
4	.735
5	.681

See appendix for additional tables. The selection of a discount rate should coincide with the company's objective as previously discussed, such as the cost of capital, corporate rate of return, industry averages, etc. This rate will serve as the cut-off, or minimum rate, at which capital investments would be considered acceptable.

Reciprocal

Since discounting is the reverse of compounding, it can be stated that compound interest rates and the present value factors are reciprocal to each other. By knowing any one factor for a given period, it is possible to calculate the other factor. This is illustrated below by the fact that both compound factors and present values reciprocate each other, and result in a total of 1 when multiplied by each other.

| | | **Interest Rate at 8%** | | |
Number of Periods	**Compound Factors**	×	**Present Values**	=	**Reciprocal**
0	1.000		1.000		1
1	1.080		.926		1
2	1.166		.857		1
3	1.260		.794		1
4	1.360		.735		1
5	1.469		.681		1

DCF Calculations

There are two generally accepted methods of computing DCF. Both methods result in the same decision, but are approached differently. One is the internal rate of return method (IRR), and the other is the net present value method (NPV). The following will illustrate both methods.

Internal rate of return (IRR)—This method will compute that interest rate which discounts the projected cash flows to equal the initial investment. This method requires a trial and error, and generally results in interpolating the results. Given the following cash flows, what DCF rate will equal the initial investment of $25,000?

Year	Cash Flows	DCF at 10% Factor	DCF at 10% Present Values	DCF at 20% Factor	DCF at 20% Present Values	DCF at 15% Factor	DCF at 15% Present Values
1	$10,000	.909	$ 9,090	.833	$ 8,330	.870	$ 8,700
2	9,000	.826	7,434	.694	6,246	.756	6,804
3	8,000	.751	6,008	.579	4,632	.658	5,264
4	7,000	.683	4,781	.482	3,374	.572	4,004
5	6,000	.621	3,726	.402	2,412	.497	2,982
	$40,000		31,039		24,994		27,754
Less initial investment			25,000		25,000		25,000
Net present values			$ 6,039		$ (6)		$ 2,754

In this illustration, the IRR is approximately 20%. At the 10% and 15% discount rates, the net present values exceed the investment by $6,039, and $2,754, respectively. However, at the 20% rate, a negative of $6 remains, which indicates that the discount rate which equals the initial investment is approximately 20%.

Net present value method (NPV)—This method uses a given discount rate in keeping with corporate objectives, and computes the net present values of the projected cash flows. The net present values are then interpreted as follows:

if the net present values are positive, the capital investment is anticipated to be profitable.

if the net present values are negative, it is anticipated the investment will generate an unfavorable profit, insufficient to recover the original investment.

Using the cash flow data previously presented at a 15% discount rate, the following net present values result.

	DCF at 15%		
	Cash		Present
Year	Flows	Factor	Values
1	$10,000.	.870	$ 8,700
2	9,000	.756	6,804
3	8,000	.658	5,264
4	7,000	.572	4,004
5	6,000	.497	2,982
	$40,000		27,754
Less initial investment			25,000
Net present values			$ 2,754

This project results in a positive net present value; therefore, it would be accepted. However, it must be compared to other projects, which may, in fact, produce a higher net present value. At this point, determination must be made as to what projects will be approved in light of the financial position of the company.

Excess present value index (EPV)—another variation of DCF uses net present values, and is expressed in the form of an index. Its primary use is to put investments of different types and levels on an equal basis for ranking purposes. Assuming the option existed whereby the $25,000 investment could be spent as one project of $25,000, or two separate projects of $12,500, what are the excess present value indexes?

	Proposed Investment	Alternatives	
		1	2
Investment	$25,000	$12,500	$12,500
Net present values	27,754	13,877	13,877
Excess present values	$ 2,754	$ 1,377	$ 1,377
EPV index	1.110	1.110	1.110

Both situations result in the same excess present values and EPV index. There-fore, the option is open as to a total investment of $25,000, or two investments of $12,500.

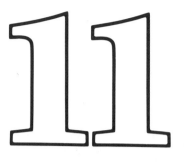

REPORTING STRATEGIES

The accounting system measures results in accordance with generally accepted accounting principles. These principles represent the practices, rules, and procedures used in the preparation of financial statements at a particular point in time. They were developed based on experiences of businesses, which reflected the custom of the industry in which the business operates. Since business practices change, these principles change by responding to the needs of the users, such as management, creditors, investors, regulatory agencies, etc.

The accounting system is generally patterned after generally accepted accounting practices. Within these confines, businesses will establish additional recording of financial activities as to the make-up of the company, such as organizational lines, which would include the personality and the chemistry of the company. Therefore, it can be said that the accounting system is comprised of various sets of activities, both human and fixed resources, and sets of financial data.

From accounting data information is provided to indicate how well the business is performing. This is measured against budgeted expectations and/or prior period performance, such as last month, last quarter, or last year. From analyzing these results problem areas will surface that need attention, and specific decisions will be made to further maximize favorable areas of the business, and to minimize unfavorable areas. By this process of evaluation, companies will be assured that adequate resources are made available and utilized in obtaining desired objectives.

REPORTING SYSTEMS

Reporting and control systems provide the mechanism whereby communications are established between individuals as to what is expected, that is, budget standards, and how did performance measure up to what was expected, or actual results. It is through this process that performance standards are established, and performance measurement results evaluated. It is also a tool which managers can use to appraise and motivate subordinates to ultimately reach those programs and goals established by the business.

A good reporting system will have standards in which performance can be measured. These standards, such as budgets, must be capable of being measured on a frequent and continuous basis. Not providing this measurement device will not allow any corrective actions to be taken when deviations result from established standards. One of the main purposes of a financial reporting system is to highlight areas of deficiency, so that corrective actions can be taken, and tasks assigned to the responsible individual(s). This process can only take place effectively when financial activities are measured against some planned objective.

TYPES OF CONTROL SYSTEMS

As previously discussed, various business segments can be established to measure performance. It is important that these segments be reviewed, since reports will be designed in keeping with organizational and/or functional lines.

- □ *Cost centers*—this segment measures output in terms of predetermined costs, such as a manufacturing plant's output, where costs are measured against predetermined standards.
- □ *Expense centers*—generally measured by organizational units, such as overhead centers, i.e., accounting functions, administrative departments, etc.
- □ *Investment centers*—measures the investment necessary to produce a stated amount of earnings.
- □ *Profit centers*—both revenues and expenses are measured, and the relationship between them results as a profit.
- □ *Revenue centers*—measures performance in terms of sales revenues, such as a sales or marketing department.

To effectively have a good reporting system for management, it is important that certain basics be followed. While these basics are general in nature, the design and execution should follow the chemistry and organizational structure of the area(s) to be evaluated. Later discussions will deal with the types of reports needed. Most good reports will fall into one of the following categories.

Organizational lines—As previously discussed, reports should follow organization structure to measure performance, such as budget vs. actual. These reports should be designed so that responsibility centers can be measured, and preferably, measured as to where responsibility centers also have authority and control over the activity of the center.

Timeliness—Reports must be timely for responsibility centers to react to changing conditions of the business. Since reports enable the user to make decisions, timeliness is paramount in carrying out this function. Different reports, responsibility centers, companies, and industries, will have a uniqueness as to the timeliness of various reports. This should be established in advance and time schedules developed and adhered to.

Elimination of excessive reports—This is a problem that concerns many organizations. There are several ways of eliminating this problem. One way is to consider the cost of each report, and attempt to weigh the cost in relation to the benefit. Employ a method of exception reporting, whereby only exceptions are reported, and not the overall data. Keep reports in summary form, with only support where necessary, and on an exception basis only. Carefully screen distribution lists, and periodically check to see if the users still need to continue receiving appropriate reports. Good report design will also eliminate excessive reports, whereby several reports may be designed into one more meaningful report. Remember, the cost of paper, preparation, and the user's time, may be counterproductive if caution is not taken to remedy excessive reporting.

Clarity of reports—A clear and meaningful report must be presented in some logical sequence, such as, what are the significant problems, remedies to solve these problems, and the effect of actions taken. Reports must be well written with reliability and accuracy. Errors create lack of confidence. When reports contain figures, such as financial reports, they need to contain comparative data. This will give the user the ability to measure performance to set goals, and to develop trends within the business. Such comparative data may include actual vs. budget, this year vs. last year, etc. When issuing a financial report, a commentary is recommended which will explain or interpret the data. By doing this, the reader will be directed to focus on the main areas that the report is being directed to. In general, keep reports short and easy to read.

Orientation towards user—The preparer of a report(s) must keep in mind the ultimate user(s) of the report. This will determine what form of presentation is necessary. For example, should the report contain graphs, narrative, statistics, or combinations thereof? Each user will have a preference that is in keeping with the users background and the purpose for which the presentation is being used. Therefore, reports should be designed to not only meet the needs of the user, but presented through the eyes of the user. In general, consider other forms of communicating to eliminate reports, such as meetings, telephones, and visual presentations. Eliminating unnecessary reports should be the objective of all organizations.

Types of Reports

In all organizations reports will serve different needs. Some reports are for information only. Some are needed for controlling the business, while others interpret the future through planning reports. Each report serves a different need, yet some overlap and may be used to either complement each other, or may serve more than one purpose. The types presented should only be used as guidelines to develop reports to meet the needs, chemistry, and organizational lines. It is not suggested that these are the only reports that can be developed, but merely a sampling for illustration purposes.

Data reports. These types of reports provide information for interpreting performance, and are used for analytical and trend purposes. Any report that provides such information as changes in earning statements and balance sheets, sales mix, customer analysis, product analysis, breakeven analysis, product contribution, etc., would be considered a data report. The following are examples of these types of reports.

Product Contribution Report Month, 19X1						
Product	Units	Revenue	Product Costs	Selling Costs	Other	Product Contribution

Product Analysis Report Month, 19X1	Changes Due To			
Product	Volume	Price	Cost	Total

Analysis of Materials Cost Variance Month, 19X1 Plant _____						
Material Type	Quantity Purchased	Unit Cost	Cost Per Unit			Variance
			Actual	Budget	Variance	

Accounts Receivable Analysis Month, 19X1							
Division/ Product Line	Customer Receivables	Current	Total	1-30	31-60	61-90	Over 90

Capital Expenditures Period _____						
Project #	Completion Date	% Completed	Planned Costs	Est. Costs	Actual To-Date	Variance

Operating reports. As the name implies, these reports are used in the operations and control of the business. They are used to highlight the management areas that need corrective actions, as well as for general information purposes. For example, how well did actual revenues and expenses compare to budgeted levels by company, division, product, or responsibility center? Are actual general and administrative expenses in line with budget? Are cash reports, such as cash receipts and disbursements, in keeping with need? Are inventories and receivables at workable levels? Some of these reports will result in prompt corrective action, while others will result in longer term decisions. These reports should be designed to control all of the major segments of the business in all areas, such as revenues, expenses, balance sheet items, and all supplemental data. With this information as a base, longer range planning will become more meaningful. Some of these types of reports are presented below.

Variance Report Actual versus Budget Month, 19X1						
Month			Total Company or Responsibility Unit	Year-to-Date		
Actual	Budget	Var. From Budget		Actual	Budget	Var. From Budget
			Revenues Expenses Net Earnings			

Variance Report Actual versus Budget Month, 19X1						
Month				Year-to-Date		
Actual	Budget	Var. From Budget	Region	Actual	Budget	Var. From Budget
			Revenues Expenses Regional Contribution			

Sources and Uses of Funds Period Ended _____	
	Amounts
Cash balance—beginning of period Funds generated from: Funds used for: Net increase (decrease) Cash balance—end of period	

Planning reports. These reflect anticipated activities at some later date. They may represent the short-range, such as one year or less, or the long-range, more than one year. These reports would overlap both data and operations reports, since both of these types of reports would measure performance against a planned standard. They would cover all segments of the company, as well as the entire company's operations. Such reports as earnings and balance sheet projections, capital needs, cash flow forecasts, product and market data, marketing forecasts, and general and administrative expenses, would represent just some of the types of reports needed for planning the future activities of the operation.

Need for Information

Reports are determined by the need for information. This information will vary by the nature and operating strategy of the company. Many companies operate most effectively with few reports, while others require many. As a user of reports, it is important to determine the need for information, and what types of reports are needed to effectively operate the business. The following are some questions that must be answered to determine these needs.

based on the decisions I need to make regularly, what facts do I need in preference order and how regularly?

to what extent do I need accuracy?

how do I wish to receive this data, such as charts, memos, computer reports, meetings, or by telephone?

what other individuals need this information, and therefore, require this report?
do the costs of preparing this report outweigh the benefits?
how important are the reports I am currently receiving?
by what mechanism can I review these reports and how often?

SUMMARY

In summary, providing the basics for good reporting will provide the necessary ingredients for decision-making. To effectively manage a business, information must be available. It must be available in the form that best fits the needs of the decision-maker. Accurate, timely, and meaningful reports are a must in any well-managed organization.

APPENDICES

Present Value Tables

Years	1%	2%	4%	6%	8%	10%	12%	14%
1	0.990	0.980	0.962	0.943	0.926	0.909	0.893	0.877
2	0.980	0.961	0.925	0.890	0.857	0.826	0.797	0.769
3	0.971	0.942	0.889	0.840	0.794	0.751	0.712	0.675
4	0.961	0.924	0.855	0.792	0.735	0.683	0.636	0.592
5	0.951	0.906	0.822	0.747	0.681	0.621	0.567	0.519
6	0.942	0.888	0.790	0.705	0.630	0.564	0.507	0.456
7	0.933	0.871	0.760	0.665	0.583	0.513	0.452	0.400
8	0.923	0.853	0.731	0.627	0.540	0.467	0.404	0.351
9	0.914	0.837	0.703	0.592	0.500	0.424	0.361	0.308
10	0.905	0.820	0.676	0.558	0.463	0.386	0.322	0.270
11	0.896	0.804	0.650	0.527	0.429	0.350	0.287	0.237
12	0.887	0.788	0.625	0.497	0.397	0.319	0.257	0.208
13	0.879	0.773	0.601	0.469	0.368	0.290	0.229	0.182
14	0.870	0.758	0.577	0.442	0.340	0.263	0.205	0.160
15	0.861	0.743	0.555	0.417	0.315	0.239	0.183	0.140
16	0.853	0.728	0.534	0.394	0.292	0.218	0.163	0.123
17	0.844	0.714	0.513	0.371	0.270	0.198	0.146	0.108
18	0.836	0.700	0.494	0.350	0.250	0.180	0.130	0.095
19	0.828	0.686	0.475	0.331	0.232	0.164	0.116	0.083
20	0.820	0.673	0.456	0.312	0.215	0.149	0.104	0.073
21	0.811	0.660	0.439	0.294	0.199	0.135	0.093	0.064
22	0.803	0.647	0.422	0.278	0.184	0.123	0.083	0.056
23	0.795	0.634	0.406	0.262	0.170	0.112	0.074	0.049
24	0.788	0.622	0.390	0.247	0.158	0.102	0.066	0.043
25	0.780	0.610	0.375	0.233	0.146	0.092	0.059	0.038
26	0.772	0.598	0.361	0.220	0.135	0.084	0.053	0.033
27	0.764	0.586	0.347	0.207	0.125	0.076	0.047	0.029
28	0.757	0.574	0.333	0.196	0.116	0.069	0.042	0.026
29	0.749	0.563	0.321	0.185	0.107	0.063	0.037	0.022
30	0.742	0.552	0.308	0.174	0.099	0.057	0.033	0.020

Present Value Tables (Continued)

Years	15%	16%	18%	20%	22%	24%	25%	26%
1	0.870	0.862	0.847	0.833	0.820	0.806	0.800	0.794
2	0.756	0.743	0.718	0.694	0.672	0.650	0.640	0.630
3	0.658	0.641	0.609	0.579	0.551	0.524	0.512	0.500
4	0.572	0.552	0.516	0.482	0.451	0.423	0.410	0.397
5	0.497	0.476	0.437	0.402	0.370	0.341	0.328	0.315
6	0.432	0.410	0.370	0.335	0.303	0.275	0.262	0.250
7	0.376	0.354	0.314	0.279	0.249	0.222	0.210	0.198
8	0.327	0.305	0.266	0.233	0.204	0.179	0.168	0.157
9	0.284	0.263	0.225	0.194	0.167	0.144	0.134	0.125
10	0.247	0.227	0.191	0.162	0.137	0.116	0.107	0.099
11	0.215	0.195	0.162	0.135	0.112	0.094	0.086	0.079
12	0.187	0.168	0.137	0.112	0.092	0.076	0.069	0.062
13	0.163	0.145	0.116	0.093	0.075	0.061	0.055	0.050
14	0.141	0.125	0.099	0.078	0.062	0.049	0.044	0.039
15	0.123	0.108	0.084	0.065	0.051	0.040	0.035	0.031
16	0.107	0.093	0.071	0.054	0.042	0.032	0.028	0.025
17	0.093	0.080	0.060	0.045	0.034	0.026	0.023	0.020
18	0.081	0.069	0.051	0.038	0.028	0.021	0.018	0.016
19	0.070	0.060	0.043	0.031	0.023	0.017	0.014	0.012
20	0.061	0.051	0.037	0.026	0.019	0.014	0.012	0.010
21	0.053	0.044	0.031	0.022	0.015	0.011	0.009	0.008
22	0.046	0.038	0.026	0.018	0.013	0.009	0.007	0.006
23	0.040	0.033	0.022	0.015	0.010	0.007	0.006	0.005
24	0.035	0.028	0.019	0.013	0.008	0.006	0.005	0.004
25	0.030	0.024	0.016	0.010	0.007	0.005	0.004	0.003
26	0.026	0.021	0.014	0.009	0.006	0.004	0.003	0.002
27	0.023	0.018	0.011	0.007	0.005	0.003	0.002	0.002
28	0.020	0.016	0.010	0.006	0.004	0.002	0.002	0.002
29	0.017	0.014	0.008	0.005	0.003	0.002	0.002	0.001
30	0.015	0.012	0.007	0.004	0.003	0.002	0.001	0.001

Present Value Tables (Continued)

Years	28%	30%	35%	40%	45%	50%
1	0.781	0.769	0.741	0.714	0.690	0.667
2	0.610	0.592	0.549	0.510	0.476	0.444
3	0.477	0.455	0.406	0.364	0.328	0.296
4	0.373	0.350	0.301	0.260	0.226	0.198
5	0.291	0.269	0.223	0.186	0.156	0.132
6	0.227	0.207	0.165	0.133	0.108	0.088
7	0.178	0.159	0.122	0.095	0.074	0.059
8	0.139	0.123	0.091	0.068	0.051	0.039
9	0.108	0.094	0.067	0.048	0.035	0.026
10	0.085	0.073	0.050	0.035	0.024	0.017
11	0.066	0.056	0.037	0.025	0.017	0.012
12	0.052	0.043	0.027	0.018	0.012	0.008
13	0.040	0.033	0.020	0.013	0.008	0.005
14	0.032	0.025	0.015	0.009	0.006	0.003
15	0.025	0.020	0.011	0.006	0.004	0.002
16	0.019	0.015	0.008	0.005	0.003	0.002
17	0.015	0.012	0.006	0.003	0.002	0.001
18	0.012	0.009	0.005	0.002	0.001	0.001
19	0.009	0.007	0.003	0.002	0.001	
20	0.007	0.005	0.002	0.001	0.001	
21	0.006	0.004	0.002	0.001		
22	0.004	0.003	0.001	0.001		
23	0.003	0.002	0.001			
24	0.003	0.002	0.001			
25	0.002	0.001	0.001			
26	0.002	0.001				
27	0.001	0.001				
28	0.001	0.001				
29	0.001	0.001				
30	0.001					

Compound Tables

Year	1%	2%	3%	4%	5%	6%	7%
1	1.010	1.020	1.030	1.040	1.050	1.060	1.070
2	1.020	1.040	1.061	1.082	1.102	1.124	1.145
3	1.030	1.061	1.093	1.125	1.156	1.191	1.225
4	1.041	1.082	1.126	1.170	1.216	1.262	1.311
5	1.051	1.104	1.159	1.217	1.276	1.338	1.403
6	1.062	1.120	1.194	1.265	1.340	1.419	1.501
7	1.072	1.149	1.230	1.316	1.407	1.504	1.606
8	1.083	1.172	1.267	1.369	1.477	1.594	1.718
9	1.094	1.195	1.305	1.423	1.551	1.689	1.838
10	1.105	1.219	1.344	1.480	1.629	1.791	1.967
11	1.116	1.243	1.384	1.539	1.710	1.898	2.105
12	1.127	1.268	1.426	1.601	1.796	2.012	2.252
13	1.138	1.294	1.469	1.665	1.886	2.133	2.410
14	1.149	1.319	1.513	1.732	1.980	2.261	2.579
15	1.161	1.346	1.558	1.801	2.079	2.397	2.759
16	1.173	1.373	1.605	1.873	2.183	2.540	2.952
17	1.184	1.400	1.653	1.948	2.292	2.693	3.159
18	1.196	1.428	1.702	2.026	2.407	2.854	3.380
19	1.208	1.457	1.754	2.107	2.527	3.026	3.617
20	1.220	1.486	1.806	2.191	2.653	3.207	3.870
25	1.282	1.641	2.094	2.666	3.386	4.292	5.427
30	1.348	1.811	2.427	3.243	4.322	5.743	7.612

Compound Tables (Continued)

Year	8%	9%	10%	12%	14%	15%	16%
1	1.080	1.090	1.100	1.120	1.140	1.150	1.160
2	1.166	1.188	1.210	1.254	1.300	1.322	1.346
3	1.260	1.295	1.331	1.405	1.482	1.521	1.561
4	1.360	1.412	1.464	1.574	1.689	1.749	1.811
5	1.469	1.539	1.611	1.762	1.925	2.011	2.100
6	1.587	1.677	1.772	1.974	2.195	2.313	2.436
7	1.714	1.828	1.949	2.211	2.502	2.660	2.826
8	1.851	1.993	2.144	2.476	2.853	3.059	3.278
9	1.999	2.172	2.358	2.773	3.252	3.518	3.803
10	2.159	2.367	2.594	3.106	3.707	4.046	4.411
11	2.332	2.580	2.853	3.479	4.226	4.652	5.117
12	2.518	2.813	3.138	3.896	4.818	5.350	5.936
13	2.720	3.066	3.452	4.363	5.492	6.153	6.886
14	2.937	3.342	3.797	4.887	6.261	7.076	7.988
15	3.172	3.642	4.177	5.474	7.138	8.137	9.266
16	3.426	3.970	4.595	6.130	8.137	9.358	10.748
17	3.700	4.328	5.054	6.866	9.276	10.761	12.468
18	3.996	4.717	5.560	7.690	10.575	12.375	14.463
19	4.316	5.142	6.116	8.613	12.056	14.232	16.777
20	4.661	5.604	6.728	9.646	13.743	16.367	19.461
25	6.848	8.632	10.835	17.000	26.462	32.919	40.874
30	10.063	13.268	17.449	29.960	50.950	66.212	85.850

Compound Tables (Continued)

Year	18%	20%	24%	28%	32%	40%	50%
1	1.180	1.200	1.240	1.280	1.320	1.400	1.500
2	1.392	1.440	1.538	1.638	1.742	1.960	2.250
3	1.643	1.728	1.907	2.067	2.300	2.744	3.375
4	1.939	2.074	2.364	2.684	3.036	3.842	5.062
5	2.288	2.488	2.932	3.436	4.007	5.378	7.594
6	2.700	2.986	3.635	4.398	5.290	7.530	11.391
7	3.185	3.583	4.508	5.629	6.983	10.541	17.086
8	3.759	4.300	5.590	7.206	9.217	14.758	25.629
9	4.435	5.160	6.931	9.223	12.166	20.661	38.443
10	5.234	6.192	8.594	11.806	16.060	28.925	57.665
11	6.176	7.430	10.657	15.112	21.199	40.496	86.498
12	7.288	8.916	13.215	19.343	27.983	56.694	129.746
13	8.599	10.699	16.386	24.759	36.937	79.372	194.619
14	10.147	12.839	20.319	31.691	48.757	111.120	291.929
15	11.074	15.407	25.196	40.565	64.350	155.568	437.894
16	14.129	18.488	31.243	51.923	84.954	217.795	656.84
17	16.672	22.186	38.741	66.461	112.14	304.914	985.26
18	19.673	26.623	48.039	85.071	148.02	426.879	1477.9
19	23.214	31.948	59.568	108.89	195.39	597.630	2216.8
20	27.393	38.338	73.864	139.38	257.92	836.683	3325.3
25	62.669	95.396	216.542	478.90	1033.6	4499.880	25251.
30	143.371	237.376	634.820	1645.5	4142.1	24201.432	191750.

GLOSSARY

ABSORPTION COSTING   Includes manufacturing costs, both variable and fixed, to all units produced.

ACCOUNTABILITY CENTER   Segments of a business for which managers have responsibility and authority to manage an operation. Also referred to as a responsibility center.

ACCOUNTABILITY MANAGEMENT   Concept whereby both responsibility and authority are given to carry out functions of an organization.

ACCOUNTING METHOD   An evaluation technique which measures capital investment proposals using accounting data.

ACCOUNTING RATE OF RETURN METHOD   See accounting method.

ACCOUNTING SYSTEM   Measures results in accordance with generally accepted accounting principles.

ACCOUNTS RECEIVABLE TO WORKING CAPITAL   Measures the impact of accounts receivable on liquidity.

ACCUMULATED DEPRECIATION   Depreciation accumulated as of a given date on the balance sheet.

ACCUMULATED RETAINED EARNINGS STATEMENT   Reflects changes in retained earnings balance due to such additions and/or deletions as retained earnings and dividends.

ACID TEST   Measures ability to meet current obligations by placing emphasis on liquid assets.

ACTUAL COSTS   Include both acquisition and historical costs.

ADJUSTED INCOME METHOD   A type of cash budget which adjusts net earnings to a cash basis.

ADMINISTRATIVE BUDGET   Reflects all expenses of administrative departments.

APPLICATION OF FUNDS   Increase assets and decreases liabilities and net worth.

APPROXIMATE RATE OF RETURN   See accounting method.

BALANCE SHEET   A financial statement which represents what a company owns and owes to others at a particular point in time.

BOOK VALUE RATE OF RETURN METHOD   See accounting method.

BOTTOM-UP BUDGETING   A budgeting approach that begins at the operating level, and is built-up at each upward level of the organization.

BREAKEVEN   Activity level where revenues and costs are in balance.

BREAKEVEN POINT   When net sales equal both variable and fixed costs.

BUDGET   Formal expression of the plans and objectives of management, covering all phases of operations for a specific period of time.

BUDGETING   The entire process of budget preparation, including planning, review, monitoring, and reporting process.

CAPITAL EXPENDITURES BUDGET   Represents a process by which proposed capital investments are formally presented.

CAPITAL SURPLUS   Amount over the par or legal value of the stock paid-in by the shareholders.

CASH BUDGET   Provides data on monies to be received and monies to be paid out.

CASH FLOW   Represents net earnings plus depreciation as used in capital investment evaluations.

CASH RECEIPTS AND DISBURSEMENTS METHOD   A type of cash budget which projects classifications of cash receipts and cash disbursements.

CASH RECOVERY PERIOD METHOD   See payback method.

COMPOUNDING   The value of money is shifted from the present into the future.

CONTRIBUTION PRICING   Utilizes the breakeven concept by establishing prices in keeping with volume levels, fixed costs, and desired profits.

COST CENTERS   Measures output in terms of predetermined costs.

COST OF SALES TO INVENTORIES   Measures turnover of inventories.

COST PRICE VARIANCE   Measures changes in cost of sales due to changes in the cost of the product.

COST REDUCTION PROJECTS   Projects where cost savings can be justified and measured.

COST VOLUME VARIANCE   Changes in units sold between periods.

CURRENT ASSETS   Assets convertible into cash within one year from the date of the issued balance sheet.

CURRENT LIABILITIES   Obligations that are to be paid, or fall due within the present operating year.

CURRENT LIABILITIES TO TANGIBLE NET WORTH   Measures the degree of protection provided by the owners to short-term creditors.

CURRENT RATIO   General indication of the ability to meet current obligations.

DATA REPORTS   Provide information for interpreting performance, and are used for analytical and trend purposes.

DAYS SALES IN TOTAL CURRENT LIABILITIES   Measures the number of days sales needed to meet current liabilities.

DAYS SALES ON HAND   Measures the average length of time inventory is held before sale.

DAYS SALES OUTSTANDING   Indicates the control over collections by measuring the age of accounts receivable.

DEBT TO EQUITY   Extent to which a company is financed by both borrowed and contributed capital.

DEFERRED CHARGES   Expenditures for which benefits will be received over future years.

DIRECT COSTING   Allocates variable costs to the product. Fixed costs treated as period expenses.

DISCOUNTED CASH FLOW (DCF)   A capital evaluation technique which uses the interest rate to determine percentage return that an investor may expect on those funds to be recovered.

DISCOUNTED PAYBACK PERIOD METHOD   Evaluation technique of payback which applies discounted cash flow factors.

DISCOUNTING   The value of money to be received in the future is shifted back to the present.

EARNINGS STATEMENT   Financial statement representing the activity in operating the business reflecting revenues and all costs.

EXCESS PRESENT VALUE INDEX (EPV)   A variation of DCF which uses net present values, and is expressed in the form of an index.

EXPENSE CENTERS   Measured along organizational lines.

EXTERNAL MEASUREMENT   Measuring performance outside the internal organization, such as competitive industries.

FINANCIAL PRICING   Pricing which considers the relationship between volume, cost, and price.

FINANCIAL RATIO MATRIX   Summation of ratios reflecting various impacts on financial statements.

FIXED COSTS   Not directly related to rate of output.

FORECAST   Projection of activity for a specified period of time.

FULL COSTING   See absorption costing.

FUNDS EMPLOYED   Total assets less current liabilities.

GENERALLY ACCEPTED ACCOUNTING PRINCIPLES   Represent the practices, rules, and procedures used in the preparation of financial statements at a particular point in time.

GROSS MARGIN   Net sales less the cost of sales.

GROSS MARGIN PERCENT   Gross margin as a percent of net sales.

GROSS MARGIN TO NET SALES   Measures the margin percentage of sales over the cost of sales.

GROWTH AND EXPANSION PROJECTS   Projects that produce earnings and contain substantial risks.

HIGH PRICE PRICING   Establishing higher than usual prices on selected products.

HUMAN RESOURCE BUDGET   Details human resource requirements such as headcount, salaries and wages, and employee benefits.

IN AND OUT PRICING   Products priced at a high value, and price reductions instituted when the segment of the market sought after becomes saturated.

INTANGIBLES   Non-physical assets having value to a company.

INTEREST RATE OF RETURN   See discounted cash flow.

INTERNAL MEASUREMENT   Measuring internal performance, such as divisions, investment centers, profit centers, and product lines.

INTERNAL RATE OF RETURN (IRR)   A method of capital evaluation that solves for the interest rate which discounts the projected cash flows to equal the initial investment.

INVENTORIES TO WORKING CAPITAL   Measures inventory balances to working capital.

INVENTORY TURNOVER   Highlights excessive inventory.

INVESTMENT CENTERS   Considers both elements of earnings and investment. It measures the necessary support of investment to produce earnings.

INVESTOR'S METHOD   See discounted cash flow.

JOB ORDER COSTING   Accumulates costs of an identifiable product known as a job, and follows the product through the production stages.

LIQUIDITY RATIO   Ability to convert assets into cash to meet current obligations.

LONG-TERM DEBT   Obligations not due in current period, or due after one year.

LONG-TERM DEBT TO WORKING CAPITAL   Measures the contribution by creditors to the working funds of the company.

MANAGING RATIOS   Evaluates segments of the balance sheet.

MANUFACTURING BUDGET   Reflects all costs of manufacturing a product, namely, material, labor, and overhead.

MARGIN OF SAFETY   Actual sales minus sales at breakeven.

MARGINAL EFFICIENCY OF CAPITAL   See discounted cash flow.

MARGINAL INCOME   Available dollars to cover fixed costs after deducting variable costs.

MARGINAL INCOME RATIO   Marginal income as a percent of net sales.

MARKET PRICE OF STOCK TO NET EARNINGS PER SHARE   Referred to as the price-earnings ratio, and measures investor confidence.

MARK-UP PRICING   A financial pricing approach which makes no provision for the impact on profit of fixed costs.

NET EARNINGS PER COMMON SHARE   Per share return to common shareholders.

NET EARNINGS TO NET SALES   Measures profitability of net sales.

NET EARNINGS TO SHAREHOLDERS' EQUITY   Rate of earnings on owners' capital invested in the business.

NET EARNINGS TO TANGIBLE NET WORTH   Measures the ability to provide dividends and potential growth from net earnings.

NET EARNINGS TO TOTAL ASSETS   Measures earning capacity and operating efficiency.

NET EARNINGS TO WORKING CAPITAL   Ability to meet fund requirements for day-to-day operations.

NET FIXED ASSETS   Physical assets that are used to carry out the plans of the company.

NET FIXED ASSETS TO TANGIBLE NET WORTH   Extent to which owners' contributed capital is invested in net fixed assets.

NET PRESENT VALUE (NPV)   See discounted cash flow.

NET PRESENT VALUE METHOD   A capital evaluation method that uses a given discount rate in keeping with corporate objectives, by computing the net present values of the projected cash flows.

NET SALES TO ACCOUNTS RECEIVABLES   Measures turnover of accounts receivable.

NET SALES TO INVENTORIES   Measurement for comparing inventories in stock to sales.

NET SALES TO TANGIBLE NET WORTH   Indicates the turnover of invested capital.

NET WORKING CAPITAL   Difference between current assets and current liabilities.

OPERATING BUDGET   An estimate of activity, including revenues, expenses, and other elements, usually for the current period of operation.

OPERATING EXPENSES TO NET SALES   Measures operating efficiency.

OPERATING PROFIT   Net sales less operating expenses.

OPERATIONS REPORT   Used to control and report on the operations by highlighting areas necessary to manage the business.

OPPORTUNITY COST   Represents a benefit that is foregone as a result of not using another alternative.

OUT-OF-POCKET COSTS   Require cash outlays currently, or in the future.

PAYBACK METHOD   An evaluation technique which measures recoverability of cash by utilizing cash flow projections.

PAYBACK PERIOD METHOD   See payback method.

PAYOFF   See payback method.

PAYOUT   See payback method.

PAYOUT RATIO   Measures the amount of dividends paid from net earnings.

PERFORMANCE RATIOS   Reviews overall performance of a company.

PERIOD COSTS   Charged against revenue in the period in which the expense was incurred.

PHYSICAL ASSETS   Tangible assets needed to support the production of goods and services.

PLANNING REPORTS   Reports representing the planning activity of the company.

PRESENT WORTH   See discounted cash flow.

PRICE-EARNINGS RATIO   Reflects investor confidence by raising or lowering the multiple. High confidence, high multiple. Low confidence, low multiple.

PROCESS COSTING   Accumulates costs by a process, or operation, as it flows through production.

PRODUCT CONTRIBUTION   Product profitability by using only costs identifiable to a particular product.

PRODUCT COSTS   A manufacturing cost relating to the product. Relates to revenue in the period in which the product was sold.

PROFIT CENTERS   Measures performance of revenues and expenses, and the relationship resulting in a profit.

PROFIT CONTRIBUTION RATIO   Contribution margin divided by net sales.

PROFITABILITY INDEX   See discounted cash flow.

PROFITABILITY RATE   Measures the profit return for every dollar of sales.

PROFITABILITY RATIOS   Measures the operations by evaluating segments of the earning statement.

PSYCHOLOGICAL PRICING   Pricing just below the next dollar amount.

QUICK RATIO   See acid test.

RATE OF RETURN   A measurement tool which establishes acceptable levels of activity.

RATIOS   Used to show relationships and trends between sets of financial data.

RECIPROCAL   Reverse of compounding is discounting.

REPLACEMENT PROJECTS   Projects needed to continue or maintain the business, dependent upon potential loss of earnings.

REPORTING SYSTEMS   Provide the mechanism where communications are established between individuals as to what is expected, and how did actual results compare.

RESPONSIBILITY CENTER   Similar to accountability center.

RETAINED EARNINGS   Earnings retained in the business that have accumulated after dividends.

RETURN ON CONTROLLABLE ASSETS   Ratio measuring performance using product contribution and controllable assets.

RETURN ON INVESTMENT   A generic term which measures performance by expressing the results in the form of a ratio.

RETURN ON TOTAL ASSETS   A ratio which measures earnings produced from total assets used to generate and/or support level of earnings.

REVENUE CENTERS   Measures performance in terms of sales revenues.

SALES BUDGET   Represents all segments of revenue anticipated by the company.

SALES PRICE VARIANCE   Changes in net sales due to differing unit sales prices between periods.

SALES VOLUME VARIANCE   Changes in net sales due to changes in units sold from one period to another.

SCIENTIFIC METHOD   See discounted cash flow.

SELLING EXPENSES TO NET SALES   Measures the cost of selling a product.

SHAREHOLDERS' EQUITY   Represents the equity interest that owners have in the business.

SHAREHOLDERS' EQUITY TO TOTAL ASSETS   Amount of borrowed resources obtained from owner's contribution.

SHORT-TERM DEBT TO INVENTORIES   Measures the extent to which a company relies on funds from selling inventories on hand to meet debts.

SOURCE AND APPLICATION OF FUNDS   Reflects the flow of money by highlighting where cash was used and where cash was spent.

SOURCE OF FUNDS   Decreases assets and increases liabilities and net worth.

STANDARD COSTS   Anticipated or predetermined costs of producing a unit of output.

TARGET RATES   An objective or criteria for measuring acceptable or unacceptable levels of activity.

TIME ADJUSTED RATE OF RETURN   See discounted cash flow.

TOP-DOWN BUDGETING   A budgeting approach that establishes corporate goals and budgets by a central corporate staff.

TOTAL DEBT TO TANGIBLE NET WORTH   Measures the amount of equity creditors have in the assets in relation to the owners.

TURNOVER RATE   Measured by compounding net sales as a percent of investment.

TYPICAL PRICING   Regarded by customer as being a typical price for the product.

UNADJUSTED RATE OF RETURN   See accounting method.

UNIT CONTRIBUTION MARGIN   Contribution margin divided by unit volume.

VARIABLE CONTRIBUTION   Net sales less variable costs.

VARIABLE COSTS   Costs that fluctuate directly with volume changes.

VOLUME COVERAGE PRICING   Low margin, high volume philosophy.

WEIGHTED COST OF CAPITAL   A measurement tool representing an average rate of earnings which investors require to induce them to invest in a company, and provide the needed capital for investment purposes.

WORKING CAPITAL   Current assets less current liabilities.

WORKING CAPITAL RATIOS   Serve as indicators in appraising the working capital condition of a company.

WORKING CAPITAL TURNOVERS   Measures the activity and utilization of working capital.

INDEX